HUMAN FACTORS IN CYBERSECURITY

Understanding Behavioral Biases and Vulnerabilities

Oluomachi Eunice Ejiofor

Copyright © 2022. All rights reserved. Oluomachi Eunice Ejiofor

No part of this book may be reproduced or transmitted in any form or by any means, electronic or mechanical, including photocopying, recording, or by any information storage and retrieval system, without permission in writing from the Copyright owner.

Any information is to be used for educational and information purposes only. It should never be substituted for financial advice.

The author or publisher does not in any way endorse any commercial products or services linked from other websites to this book.

Globally Available

ISBN: 978-7-9633-9688-3

Published in Nigeria in 2022
Emphaloz Publishing House

A catalogue record of this book will be available from the National Library of Nigeria.

DEDICATION

To my family, whose unwavering support and understanding have been my anchor through countless hours of research and writing—thank you for believing in me and for being my source of strength and encouragement. Your patience and love have made this journey possible.

To the dedicated professionals in the field of cybersecurity and individuals who are curious to delve into this world: this book is a tribute to your relentless pursuit of excellence and your commitment to understanding our digital world. Your expertise and passion inspire every chapter, and I hope this work serves as both a valuable resource and a testament to your vital contributions.

PREFACE

This book examines the critical role that human behavior plays in cybersecurity. It begins by exploring the various cognitive biases and psychological factors that influence decision-making and security practices. It sheds light on how these biases can lead to security lapses and vulnerabilities, offering a foundational understanding of the human element in cyber defense.

The core of the book focuses on practical aspects of addressing human vulnerabilities, including phishing, social engineering, and the impact of stress and fatigue on security behavior. It provides insights into effective user awareness training, the influence of organizational culture, and the role of behavioral economics in shaping security practices. Through case studies and real-world examples, the book demonstrates how understanding and mitigating human factors can enhance overall security.

In its concluding sections, the book addresses the design of user-friendly security solutions and the importance of psychological resilience in building a robust defense. It also considers ethical issues related to privacy and manipulation in security awareness efforts. Human Factors in Cybersecurity offers a comprehensive exploration of how to improve security by addressing the behavioral aspects of cyber threats and creating more resilient systems.

TABLE OF CONTENTS

DEDICATION iii
PREFACE iv

CHAPTER ONE

THE ROLE OF BEHAVIOUR IN SECURITY 1
  Understanding Human Factors in Cybersecurity 2
  Behavioral Pitfalls in Cybersecurity 7
  Case Studies and Real-World Examples 14
  General Lessons Learned and Best Practices from the Case Studies 19

CHAPTER TWO

COGNITIVE BIASES AND DECISION-MAKING: HOW THEY AFFECT SECURITY CHOICES 21

CHAPTER THREE

THE PSYCHOLOGY OF RISK PERCEPTION IN CYBERSECURITY 33
  Cognitive Biases and Cybersecurity Risk Perception 33
  Emotional Responses and Cybersecurity Risk Perception 35
  Social and Cultural Influences on Cybersecurity Risk Perception 36

Risk Perception and Decision-Making in Cybersecurity 38

CHAPTER FOUR

PHISHING AND SOCIAL ENGINEERING: EXPLOITING BEHAVIORAL VULNERABILITIES 41

Understanding Phishing and Social Engineering 42

CHAPTER FIVE

THE INFLUENCE OF STRESS AND FATIGUE ON CYBERSECURITY PRACTICES 52

Understanding Stress and Fatigue 53

Organizational and Environmental Factors Contributing to Stress and Fatigue......... 56

The Role of Leadership in Addressing Stress and Fatigue 59

CHAPTER SIX

USER AWARENESS AND TRAINING: BRIDGING THE GAP BETWEEN KNOWLEDGE AND ACTION 62

What is the Human Factor in Cybersecurity.. 63

Designing Effective User Awareness and Training Programs 66

Practical Implementation of User Awareness and Training Programs 69

Overcoming Common Challenges 70

Case Studies and Success Stories 71

CHAPTER SEVEN
THE ROLE OF ORGANIZATIONAL CULTURE IN SHAPING SECURITY BEHAVIOR 73
Organizational Culture: An overview 74
Assessing and Shaping Security Culture 78

CHAPTER EIGHT
BEHAVIORAL ECONOMICS IN CYBERSECURITY 84
The Basics of Behavioral Economics 85
Decision-Making and Cybersecurity 89

CHAPTER NINE
DESIGNING USER-FRIENDLY SECURITY SOLUTIONS .. 95
The Importance of Usability in Security 96
Balancing Protection and Usability 99

CHAPTER TEN
PSYCHOLOGICAL RESILIENCE: BUILDING A STRONGER HUMAN FACTOR IN CYBER DEFENSE 105
Psychological Resilience: An Overview 106
Cultivating a Resilient Cybersecurity Culture 112
Practical Applications and Case Studies ... 114

CHAPTER ELEVE

ETHICAL CONSIDERATIONS: PRIVACY, MANIPULATION AND SECURITY AWARENESS **119**

  Privacy: Balancing Security and Personal Rights 120

  Case Studies and Examples 132

CHAPTER TWELVE

FUTURE DIRECTIONS **136**

ABOUT THE AUTHOR **143**

CHAPTER ONE:
THE ROLE OF BEHAVIOUR IN SECURITY

In the ever-changing terrain of cybersecurity, the spotlight has often shone brightly on technology and systems. Firewalls, encryption, and intrusion detection systems have been the focal points of defense strategies. However, as cyber threats become more sophisticated, it's clear that technology alone is insufficient. The human element which includes the decisions, behaviors, and interactions of individuals plays a crucial role in the security posture of any organization.

Human factors in cybersecurity encompass the ways in which human behavior impacts the effectiveness of security measures. Understanding these factors is critical, as human actions or inactions can either bolster or undermine the most robust security protocols. This chapter aims to explore the importance of human behavior in cybersecurity, examine common behavioral pitfalls, and offer strategies for mitigating human-related security risks.

Understanding Human Factors in Cybersecurity

Human factors refer to the interplay between humans and their environment, focusing on how people's actions, decisions, and interactions with technology affect outcomes. It shows how individual behaviors and organizational cultures influence the effectiveness of security measures.

The Impact of Human Behavior

Human behavior can significantly impact the effectiveness of cybersecurity. While advanced technologies can detect and mitigate threats, they often rely on users to implement and follow security protocols. Examples include password management, phishing susceptibility, and adherence to policies. Password management is a significant vulnerability in cybersecurity, as users often create weak passwords or reuse them across multiple sites. This practice makes it easier for attackers to gain unauthorized access to sensitive accounts. Weak passwords can be easily guessed or cracked using common techniques, and reused passwords mean that a breach on one site can compromise multiple accounts. Phishing susceptibility is another critical issue, where individuals may fall victim to phishing schemes that deceive them into providing sensitive information or credentials. Phishing attacks often use deceptive emails, messages, or websites to trick users into revealing personal details. Once attackers obtain this information, they can exploit it for unauthorized access or financial gain. Adherence to policies is also a common challenge faced. Employees might ignore or bypass established security policies and procedures, often due to convenience or a lack of understanding. When security policies are not followed, it can create vulnerabilities that jeopardize the entire organization's security framework. Ensuring that all employees are not only aware of but also compliant with security protocols is crucial for maintaining robust defenses against cyber threats.

The Human-Cybersecurity Interface

The interface between these two components is multifaceted. It involves several aspects. User training and awareness is a crucial component of an effective security strategy. Comprehensive security training programs can significantly enhance users' understanding of potential risks and improve their ability to recognize and respond to various threats. By educating users on best practices, potential attack vectors, and the latest security trends, organizations can foster a more security-conscious environment and reduce the likelihood of successful attacks due to human error. Behavioral economics offers valuable insights into how cognitive biases and decision-making processes influence security choices. By understanding these psychological factors, organizations can design more effective security systems and interventions. For instance, recognizing that users might be influenced by overconfidence or procrastination can lead to the development of tools and policies that nudge individuals toward safer behaviors, such as enforcing stronger password practices or more vigilant monitoring of suspicious activities. Organizational culture plays a significant role in shaping an organization's security posture. A culture that prioritizes security and encourages adherence to best practices can greatly impact overall cybersecurity effectiveness. When security is ingrained in the organizational culture, employees are more likely to follow protocols, report potential issues, and contribute to a collective effort to safeguard information. Promoting a culture of security awareness and responsibility helps create an environment where security practices are consistently upheld and continuously improved.

Psychological and Emotional Factors

Psychological and emotional factors play a significant role in security. Stress, fatigue, and personal issues can impact a person's ability to make sound security decisions. For instance, high-stress environments can impair judgment and lead to shortcuts or negligence in following security protocols. There can also be emotional manipulation. Attackers often exploit emotional triggers, such as fear or urgency, to deceive users into divulging sensitive information or making insecure choices.

User Empowerment and Ownership

Empowering users to take ownership of their cybersecurity practices can lead to more proactive and responsible behavior. Various strategies such as personal accountability and knowledge can be employed. Encouraging users to understand and take responsibility for their role in maintaining security can foster a sense of ownership and vigilance. Providing individuals with the knowledge and tools they need to protect themselves, such as understanding how to use security features effectively, can improve overall security posture.

Behavioral Analytics and Monitoring

Behavioral analytics and monitoring involve using data to understand and predict user behavior patterns, which can enhance security. This approach includes anomaly detection which involves analyzing typical user behavior and detecting deviations that might indicate potential security threats or breaches. There is also the mechanism of user behavior analytics. UBA systems can identify unusual or risky behaviors and alert security teams to potential issues before they escalate.

Human-Centric Design in Security Solutions

Designing security solutions with the human element in mind can significantly improve user compliance and effectiveness. Considerations can include usability and user experience. In usability, security tools should be designed to be user-friendly and seamlessly integrated into users' workflows to minimize resistance and errors. It is also imperative to enhance the user experience by making security processes intuitive and less intrusive, which can lead to better adherence to security practices and reduced user frustration.

Behavioral Pitfalls in Cybersecurity

Understanding common behavioral pitfalls is crucial for developing strategies to address them. For effective tactics to be developed to combat these hurdles, analyzing the frequent causes of these is essential. Some of these pitfalls include:

Cognitive Biases: This can lead to poor security decisions. Optimism bias and confirmation bias both play significant roles in influencing individuals' approach to security. Optimism bias leads users to underestimate the likelihood of a cyber-attack affecting them personally, fostering a sense of complacency and resulting in lax security practices. This overconfidence can leave systems vulnerable to breaches. Meanwhile, confirmation bias causes individuals to disregard security warnings or updates that challenge their existing beliefs or practices. As a result, they may ignore critical advice or fail to adapt to evolving threats, further compromising their security posture. Both biases contribute to a less proactive and less effective approach to safeguarding against cyber threats.

Social Engineering: Social engineering exploits human psychology to gain unauthorized access. Techniques include phishing and pretexting. In phishing, attackers send deceptive emails to trick users into divulging sensitive information. Pretexting entails attackers creating fabricated scenarios to persuade individuals to provide confidential information.

Overconfidence: Overconfidence in one's own security practices can lead to complacency. Persons might believe they are immune to attacks, resulting in risky behaviors and forfeiting essential information. They can delay or ignore software updates that could patch known vulnerabilities. They can also engage in risky online activities without adequate precautions.

Neglecting Software Updates: Many users and organizations delay or neglect software updates, which can leave systems vulnerable to known security vulnerabilities. Common issues include update fatigue and incompatibility concerns. Frequent update prompts can lead to user fatigue, resulting in missed updates and increased exposure to security risks. Users may also avoid updates due to concerns about potential software incompatibilities or disruptions to their workflow.

Insecure Use of Personal Devices: The use of personal devices aka (BYOD—Bring Your Own Device) in a professional setting can introduce security risks if not properly managed. Pitfalls of this arrangement can include lack of security controls and unregulated applications.

Personal devices may lack the same level of security controls and management as company-issued devices, increasing the risk of data breaches. Employees may install unregulated or potentially harmful applications on their personal devices, which can introduce vulnerabilities.

Poor Data Handling Practices: Improper handling of sensitive data can lead to accidental exposure or loss. Storing sensitive information in an unencrypted format increases the risk of data breaches if devices are lost or compromised. Individuals may mistakenly send sensitive data to the wrong recipient or store it in insecure locations, such as personal email accounts or unprotected cloud storage.

Over-Reliance on Security Tools: An over-reliance on security tools and technology can lead to complacency and a false sense of security. Issues include tool fatigue and false security. Relying on automated security tools can lead users to overlook the need for personal vigilance and judgment in identifying and addressing security threats. Also, assuming that security tools are foolproof can lead to neglecting other important security practices, such as regular training and awareness programs.

Failure to Report Security Incidents: Failure to promptly report security incidents or potential vulnerabilities can exacerbate the impact of a security breach. Fear of repercussions and underestimating risks are significant factors that can undermine effective cybersecurity management. Employees may hesitate to report security issues due to concerns about blame or negative consequences, which can delay response and mitigation efforts. This reluctance to come forward can leave vulnerabilities unaddressed for longer periods, exacerbating potential damage. Additionally, users often downplay the severity of security incidents, either due to a lack of understanding or a tendency to minimize the potential impact. This underestimation can result in inadequate or delayed responses, allowing threats to escalate and causing more extensive harm. Both issues contribute to a weakened security posture and highlight the need for a more supportive and informed approach to cybersecurity.

There are strategies that can be integrated to enhance human factors. Mechanisms such as training, policy design, and technology can be used to address challenges and improve its performance. Security training and awareness are crucial for helping users recognize and address cybersecurity risks effectively. Regular and comprehensive training programs play a pivotal role in this process. One effective strategy is conducting phishing simulations, which allow users to practice identifying and reporting suspicious emails in a controlled environment. These simulations help users become more adept at spotting potential threats and responding appropriately. Additionally, employing interactive learning methods, such as gamification, can significantly enhance the training experience. By incorporating engaging and interactive elements, these methods improve both learning and retention, ensuring that users are better prepared to handle real-world security challenges.

Behavioral interventions are essential for addressing cognitive biases and enhancing decision-making in cybersecurity. One effective approach is nudging, which involves designing systems and processes that guide users towards more secure behaviors. For instance, systems can be configured to encourage the creation and use of strong passwords, subtly steering users toward better security practices. Another important intervention is the implementation of feedback mechanisms. By providing users with immediate feedback on their security practices, organizations can reinforce positive behaviors and promptly correct any issues. These strategies help to mitigate the impact of cognitive biases and foster a more secure and informed user base.

Creating a security-focused organizational culture and implementing robust policies are crucial for influencing behavior and enhancing overall security. Clear policies are fundamental; they should be well-developed, communicated effectively, and easy for employees to follow. Such clarity ensures that everyone understands the security expectations and procedures. Leadership support plays a critical role as well; leaders should actively endorse and model good security practices, setting an example and fostering a culture where security awareness is prioritized. Also, establishing a well-defined incident response plan is essential. This plan should encourage prompt reporting of potential security incidents, enabling swift action and mitigation. Together, these elements help build a strong security culture and improve organizational resilience against cyber threats.

Technology can significantly enhance security by addressing human factors through various supportive measures. One approach is to design user-friendly interfaces for security tools, ensuring they are intuitive and integrate seamlessly into users' workflows. This ease of use helps minimize resistance and encourages consistent application of security practices. Additionally, implementing automated security features can further bolster protection by reducing the reliance on manual user actions. For example, password managers can automate the creation and storage of strong passwords, while two-factor authentication adds an extra layer of security with minimal user intervention. These technological solutions simplify security processes and help users maintain robust protection with less effort.

As technology and cyber threats evolve, so will the role of human factors in cybersecurity, leading to several promising future trends. One significant development is the integration of Artificial Intelligence (AI) and machine learning, which will enhance security by analyzing user behavior patterns to detect anomalies and potential threats. These technologies will also enable personalized security training tailored to individual user behaviors, improving overall effectiveness. Additionally, future security solutions are expected to prioritize an enhanced user experience while maintaining robust protection. This involves designing intuitive interfaces and seamlessly integrating security measures into everyday activities to reduce friction and encourage adherence. Ongoing research and development will be crucial in this context, exploring how emerging technologies like virtual reality and blockchain influence human behavior and cybersecurity. This continued exploration will drive the creation of more effective and adaptive security strategies.

Case Studies and Real-World Examples

We will explore some case studies of high-profile data breaches and how human factors played a role. This real-life example will aid us in understanding practically how it can play out in our everyday activity.

Case Study 1: The Target Data Breach (2013)

Incident Overview: In December 2013, Target experienced a massive data breach that compromised the personal and financial information of over 40 million customers. The breach occurred through a third-party vendor's compromised credentials.

Human Factors Involved: The attackers used stolen credentials from Target's HVAC vendor to gain access to the company's network. This incident highlighted failures in vendor management and inadequate network segmentation. The human error was primarily in the lack of rigorous security practices for third-party access and insufficient monitoring of vendor activity.

Lessons Learned: Organizations should implement strict security protocols for third-party vendors, including regular security assessments and enhanced monitoring. Effective network segmentation can limit the potential damage from compromised credentials. Educating employees and vendors on security best practices is also crucial.

Case Study 2: The Equifax Breach (2017)

Incident Overview: Equifax, one of the largest credit reporting agencies, suffered a data breach that exposed sensitive information of approximately 147 million people. The breach occurred because Equifax failed to apply a critical security patch for a known vulnerability in the Apache Struts framework.

Human Factors Involved: The breach was a result of human error in patch management. Equifax's IT team neglected to apply the security update in a timely manner, leaving the system vulnerable. Additionally, internal communication failures contributed to the delayed response.

Lessons Learned: Organizations must establish and enforce a robust patch management process to ensure timely updates of all software and systems. Regular internal audits and improved communication channels can help prevent similar oversights.

Social Engineering Attacks

Case Study 3: The Twitter Bitcoin Scam (2020)

Incident Overview: In July 2020, high-profile Twitter accounts, including those of Elon Musk and Barack Obama, were compromised to promote a Bitcoin scam. The attackers used social engineering tactics to manipulate Twitter employees into giving them access.

Human Factors Involved: The attack exploited employees' susceptibility to social engineering, including phishing and pretexting. The attackers used convincing social engineering tactics to bypass Twitter's security measures, highlighting gaps in employee training and security awareness.

Lessons Learned: Organizations need to enhance security training to help employees recognize and resist social engineering attacks. Implementing strict verification processes for account access and ensuring regular security drills can also reduce the risk of similar attacks.

Case Study 4: The Google and Facebook Phishing Scam (2013-2015)

Incident Overview: A phishing scam led to the theft of over $100 million from Google and Facebook over a two-year period. The attacker, who posed as a legitimate supplier, tricked employees into making fraudulent wire transfers.

Human Factors Involved: The scam succeeded due to insufficient verification processes and a lack of skepticism among employees. Employees failed to verify the authenticity of payment requests, demonstrating the importance of implementing rigorous approval and verification procedures.

Lessons Learned: Establishing strong verification protocols for financial transactions and encouraging a culture of skepticism towards unexpected requests can help prevent such scams. Regular training on phishing and social engineering can also enhance employees' ability to detect fraudulent activities.

Human Error in Security Protocols

Case Study 5: The Capital One Data Breach (2019)

Incident Overview: In July 2019, a misconfigured firewall led to the exposure of sensitive data from over 100 million

Capital One customers. The breach was attributed to a mistake made by an employee while configuring a cloud-based firewall.

Human Factors Involved: The breach resulted from human error in configuring security settings for cloud infrastructure. There was a failure to follow best practices for cloud security and to review configurations thoroughly.

Lessons Learned: Organizations should implement strict configuration management practices and conduct regular reviews of security settings. Automated tools for configuration management and monitoring can help catch errors before they lead to breaches.

Case Study 6: The Uber Data Breach (2016)

Incident Overview: Uber suffered a data breach in 2016, which exposed the personal information of 57 million users and drivers. Uber initially concealed the breach and only disclosed it a year later, which led to significant legal and reputational damage.

Human Factors Involved: The breach was exacerbated by poor incident handling and lack of transparency. The company's decision to conceal the breach rather than promptly report it reflected failures in crisis management and communication.

Lessons Learned: Transparency and prompt reporting of security incidents are crucial for effective breach management. Organizations should have clear incident response plans and foster a culture that encourages timely disclosure and proactive management of security issues.

General Lessons Learned and Best Practices from the Case Studies

Improving Security Training: Regular, interactive security training programs can help users recognize and respond to threats. Simulated attacks and real-world scenarios can enhance learning and preparedness.

Enhancing Incident Reporting: Creating a culture of openness where employees feel comfortable reporting security incidents without fear of repercussions is essential. Implementing straightforward reporting procedures and providing clear guidelines can facilitate timely and effective incident management.

Strengthening Third-Party Management: Organizations should develop comprehensive policies for third-party risk management, including security assessments, contractual requirements, and regular audits to ensure that vendors adhere to security best practices.

Implementing Robust Patch Management: Establishing a structured patch management process ensures timely application of security updates. Regular audits and automated tools can help identify and address vulnerabilities before they are exploited.

Human factors are a critical component of cybersecurity, influencing both the effectiveness of security measures and the overall security posture of organizations. By understanding and addressing behavioral pitfalls, implementing effective training and interventions, and leveraging technology, organizations can significantly enhance their cybersecurity efforts.

CHAPTER TWO:
COGNITIVE BIASES AND DECISION-MAKING: HOW THEY AFFECT SECURITY CHOICES

Understanding human behavior is crucial in developing holistic security strategies. While technological advancements have significantly enhanced our ability to detect and prevent cyber threats, human factors remain a critical component of effective security. Cognitive biases, which are systematic patterns of deviation from norm or rationality in judgment, play a significant role in shaping security choices and behaviors. These biases can lead to suboptimal decisions and vulnerabilities in cybersecurity. This chapter explores various cognitive biases and their impact on security decisions, providing a comprehensive understanding of how these biases influence user behavior and organizational security.

Optimism Bias

Optimism bias refers to the tendency of individuals to believe that they are less likely to experience negative events compared to others. This cognitive bias manifests in the realm of cybersecurity when users underestimate the likelihood of a cyber-attack impacting them personally. As a result, individuals may engage in less cautious behavior, such as using weak passwords or neglecting software updates, under the assumption that they are unlikely to be targeted.

This bias can lead to significant security risks. For example, a user might ignore warnings about phishing scams, thinking that they are savvy enough not to fall for such tricks. Similarly, an organization might delay implementing robust security measures, believing that it is unlikely to be the victim of a sophisticated attack. The consequence of optimism bias is a weakened security posture that can be exploited by cybercriminals.

To mitigate optimism bias, it is essential to foster a realistic understanding of security risks. This can be achieved through regular security training and awareness programs that emphasize the importance of proactive measures and highlight real-world examples of cyber incidents. Encouraging a culture of vigilance and emphasizing that no one is immune to cyber threats can help counteract the effects of optimism bias.

Confirmation Bias

This is the tendency to search for, interpret, and remember information that confirms one's preexisting beliefs or hypotheses while disregarding contradictory evidence. In the context of cybersecurity, this bias can manifest when individuals or organizations selectively focus on information that aligns with their current security practices or beliefs, ignoring warnings or updates that suggest otherwise.

For instance, an individual who believes that their current antivirus software is sufficient may disregard alerts about the need for more advanced protection, despite evidence showing that new threats are emerging. Similarly, a company with a long-standing security policy might resist adopting new practices or technologies, even when data suggests that these changes are necessary to address evolving threats.

Confirmation bias can lead to complacency and resistance to change, which are detrimental to maintaining effective security. To address this bias, it is crucial to promote an evidence-based approach to security decision-making.

Encouraging critical thinking and regular reassessment of security practices can help ensure that decisions are based on the most current and accurate information available.

Risk Perception Bias

Risk perception bias involves the distortion of an individual's perception of the probability and severity of a risk. People often perceive risks based on emotional responses or personal experiences rather than objective data. In cybersecurity, this bias can lead to misjudgments about the severity of security threats and the appropriate level of response.

For example, an individual might downplay the risk of a ransomware attack because they have not personally experienced one, even though such attacks are becoming increasingly common and severe. Similarly, an organization might prioritize certain types of threats based on recent high-profile incidents, neglecting other risks that are equally or more significant.

To counteract risk perception bias, it is important to provide users and organizations with accurate, data-driven risk assessments. Regularly updating threat intelligence and conducting comprehensive risk analyses can help ensure that security measures are aligned with the actual threat landscape, rather than being influenced by subjective perceptions.

Anchoring Bias

Anchoring bias occurs when individuals rely too heavily on the first piece of information they receive (the "anchor") when making decisions, even if that information is irrelevant or incorrect. In this context, anchoring bias can influence decision-making by causing individuals to rely on outdated or incorrect information when assessing risks or implementing security measures.

For instance, if an organization initially believes that a particular security tool is the best available option, it might continue to use that tool even if newer, more effective solutions become available. Similarly, an individual might base their understanding of security risks on an outdated training module or a single incident, rather than seeking updated information.

To mitigate anchoring bias, it is essential to encourage ongoing education and periodic review of security practices. Regularly updating security training materials, conducting audits, and seeking input from a diverse range of sources can help ensure that decisions are based on the most current and relevant information.

Herding Behavior

This refers to the tendency of individuals to follow the actions of a larger group, often without independently evaluating the situation. In cybersecurity, herding behavior can manifest when users or organizations adopt security practices simply because others are doing so, rather than based on a thorough assessment of their own needs and risks.

For example, a company might implement a particular security tool because it is popular in the industry, even if it does not address the company's specific security requirements. Similarly, individuals might adopt common security practices, such as using widely recommended password managers, without considering whether these tools are the best fit for their needs.

To address herding behavior, it is important to encourage critical evaluation and personalized security planning. Organizations should conduct thorough assessments of their security needs and select solutions that are tailored to their specific risks and requirements. Similarly, individuals should seek out information and advice that is relevant to their unique security context, rather than simply following trends.

Overconfidence Bias

Overconfidence bias occurs when individuals overestimate their knowledge, skills, or abilities, leading to an inflated sense of security. In this context, overconfidence can result in risky behavior, such as neglecting security protocols or dismissing potential threats as unlikely.

For instance, an individual who is confident in their ability to recognize phishing emails might be less cautious when dealing with unfamiliar messages, increasing the likelihood of falling victim to a scam. Similarly, an organization that believes its security measures are sufficient might overlook emerging threats or fail to implement necessary updates.

To counteract this bias, it is essential to promote a culture of humility and continuous learning. Regular security training, awareness programs, and assessments can help individuals and organizations maintain a realistic understanding of their security posture and the evolving threat landscape. Encouraging a mindset of ongoing improvement and vigilance can help mitigate the risks associated with overconfidence.

Status Quo Bias

Status quo bias is the tendency to prefer things to remain the same rather than change. In cybersecurity, this bias can lead to resistance to adopting new technologies, practices, or policies, even when such changes are necessary to address emerging threats.

For example, an organization might continue using outdated security tools or practices simply because they are familiar and have been in place for a long time. Similarly, individuals might resist changing their passwords or updating their software, even when advised to do so for improved security.

To overcome status quo bias, it is important to emphasize the benefits of change and the risks associated with maintaining outdated practices. Providing clear, evidence-based explanations for why updates or changes are necessary can help facilitate acceptance and adoption of new security measures.

Framing Effect

The framing effect refers to the way information is presented and how it influences decision-making. In cybersecurity, the framing of information can impact how individuals perceive risks and make security choices.

For example, if a security warning is framed in terms of potential loss ("You could lose your personal data") rather than potential gain ("Protect your valuable information"), it may elicit a stronger response from users. Similarly, how security policies and practices are communicated can influence their acceptance and implementation.

To mitigate the framing effect, it is important to present security information in a clear and balanced manner. Providing both positive and negative aspects of security measures, and framing information in a way that emphasizes both the risks and benefits, can help users make more informed decisions.

Self-Serving Bias

This refers to the tendency for individuals to attribute positive outcomes to their own actions and abilities, while blaming external factors for negative outcomes. This bias significantly impacts how users perceive and respond to security incidents and breaches. For example, individuals who successfully avoid phishing scams may attribute their success to their own vigilance and expertise, reinforcing their confidence in handling future threats. Conversely, if they fall victim to a cyber-attack, they may blame external factors, such as the sophistication of the attack or flaws in their security software, rather than acknowledging potential personal oversights or errors.

This bias can have detrimental effects on security behavior. Users who attribute their successes to personal skill may become complacent, underestimating the need for ongoing vigilance and adherence to security best practices. They might take unnecessary risks, believing that their personal capabilities are sufficient to manage any threat. On the other hand, individuals who blame external factors for their failures may fail to learn from their mistakes, leading to repeated errors and insufficient improvement in their security practices.

To address self-serving bias, several strategies can be employed. Encouraging self-reflection is crucial; users should be prompted to review their past security incidents and assess their responses critically. This practice helps individuals understand their role in both successful and unsuccessful outcomes, fostering a more accurate self-assessment. Providing balanced feedback is also important; feedback should acknowledge both effective actions and areas needing improvement. Highlighting specific examples of successful practices alongside constructive criticism helps users develop a nuanced understanding of their security capabilities.

Promoting accountability within organizations can further mitigate self-serving bias. Users should be encouraged to take responsibility for their actions and decisions regarding cybersecurity. Transparent reporting mechanisms and support for continuous learning and development reinforce this culture of accountability. Utilizing case studies and real-world examples can be another effective strategy. By examining both successful and failed responses to security incidents, users gain insights into the impact of various factors on security outcomes and can learn from the experiences of others.

Integrating learning opportunities into security training programs is essential as well. Providing ongoing educational resources that address common biases, including self-serving bias, and emphasizing the importance of a balanced perspective can help users develop a more comprehensive understanding of cybersecurity. Including scenarios that challenge self-serving biases and encourage critical thinking supports the development of better security practices and a more resilient approach to cybersecurity.

Understanding cognitive biases and their impact on decision-making is essential for improving cybersecurity. By recognizing how biases such as optimism bias, confirmation bias, risk perception bias, anchoring bias, herding behavior, overconfidence bias, status quo bias, self-serving and the framing effect influence security choices, organizations and individuals can take steps to mitigate these effects and make more informed, effective security decisions.

Implementing strategies such as realistic risk assessments, evidence-based decision-making, continuous education, and critical evaluation of security practices can help address the challenges posed by cognitive biases. By fostering a culture of vigilance and adaptability, organizations and individuals can enhance their cybersecurity posture and better protect against evolving threat trends.

CHAPTER THREE:
THE PSYCHOLOGY OF RISK PERCEPTION IN CYBERSECURITY

The way individuals perceive risk significantly influences their interactions with digital systems, their susceptibility to threats, and their overall security posture. This chapter briefly examines the psychology of risk perception specifically within the context of cybersecurity. By looking at cognitive biases, emotional responses, and social influences, we can better understand why people often fail to adhere to best practices and how to design more effective security interventions.

Cognitive Biases and Cybersecurity Risk Perception

Cognitive biases are systematic deviations from rationality that can lead to flawed judgments and decisions. In cybersecurity, these biases affect how individuals perceive and respond to digital threats.

Availability Heuristic: Here, the availability heuristic can lead to skewed perceptions of threat likelihood. For example, if a person recently heard about a high-profile data breach or ransomware attack, they might overestimate the frequency and severity of such incidents. This can result in an exaggerated fear of cyber threats, leading to either excessive caution (such as unnecessary overhauls of security protocols) or panic-driven decisions, which may not be effective.

Optimism Bias: Many individuals exhibit optimism bias when it comes to cybersecurity, believing that they are less likely to be targeted by cyber-attacks than others. This can lead to lax security practices, such as weak passwords or ignoring software updates. The belief that "it won't happen to me" diminishes the perceived need for stringent security measures, making systems more vulnerable to attacks.

Anchoring Bias: When individuals are exposed to initial security recommendations or threat assessments, they may anchor their perceptions to that information, even if subsequent evidence suggests a different level of risk. For instance, if an employee is informed that their company's firewall is sufficient, they may overlook newer and more sophisticated threats, assuming that their initial assessment remains valid.

Confirmation Bias: Confirmation bias can manifest in cybersecurity when individuals seek out or interpret information that confirms their preexisting beliefs about security threats. For example, if someone believes that phishing emails are always easy to spot, they might ignore warnings or training about sophisticated phishing schemes, underestimating their potential impact.

Emotional Responses and Cybersecurity Risk Perception

Emotions significantly influence risk perception and decision-making in cybersecurity contexts. Fear, anxiety, and overconfidence can all impact how individuals interact with digital security measures.

Fear and Anxiety: Fear of cyber-attacks, such as identity theft or data breaches, can lead to heightened vigilance but also may cause anxiety-driven behaviors. For example, an excessive fear of online threats might lead to overuse of security tools or avoidance of necessary online activities, impacting productivity and efficiency. Conversely, anxiety might lead individuals to engage in panic-driven actions, such as rapidly changing passwords without assessing whether the threat is genuine or focusing on low-impact security measures at the expense of more critical issues.

Overconfidence: On the other hand, overconfidence can lead to risky behaviors, such as neglecting software updates or underestimating the importance of strong password policies. Individuals who believe that their security knowledge is superior or that they are inherently safe from cyber threats may fail to recognize or act upon actual vulnerabilities.

Emotional Attachment: Emotional attachment to specific devices or services can also impact risk perception. For example, a person might avoid updating their favorite application due to perceived inconvenience or the fear of losing personal settings, even if updates are crucial for security. This emotional attachment can lead to vulnerabilities if updates are not performed regularly.

Social and Cultural Influences on Cybersecurity Risk Perception

This risk perception is also shaped by social norms, cultural beliefs, and group dynamics. Understanding these influences can help in designing more effective security interventions.

Social Norms and Group Behavior: Individuals often look to their peers and organizational culture when assessing cybersecurity practices. If a company's culture downplays the importance of security or if colleagues are lax in their security behaviors, employees might follow suit. Conversely, a strong culture of cybersecurity awareness and compliance can positively influence individuals to adhere to best practices and report potential security threats.

Cultural Beliefs: Different cultural backgrounds can influence how people perceive and respond to these risks. For instance, in cultures that emphasize privacy and individual responsibility, individuals might be more proactive in managing their digital security. In contrast, cultures that prioritize convenience or collectivism might experience resistance to stringent security measures if they are perceived as cumbersome or intrusive.

Trust in Institutions: Trust in technology providers, such as software vendors and cybersecurity firms, affects how individuals perceive and react to security risks. If users trust that their service providers are taking adequate security measures, they may be less vigilant in their personal security practices. Conversely, a lack of trust can lead to heightened suspicion and overprotective behaviors, such as excessive use of security tools or reluctance to use certain technologies.

Risk Perception and Decision-Making in Cybersecurity

Understanding how risk perception affects decision-making is critical for developing effective cybersecurity strategies. Individuals' perceptions of risk often shape their choices regarding security practices and policies.

Risk-Taking Behaviors: Misjudgment of cybersecurity risks can lead to risk-taking behaviors, such as ignoring security updates or clicking on suspicious links. For instance, individuals who underestimate the risks of malware may be more likely to download and install software from untrusted sources, increasing their vulnerability to attacks.

Risk Management Strategies: Effective risk management requires addressing both the cognitive and emotional factors influencing cybersecurity behaviors. Strategies include designing intuitive security systems, providing clear and actionable risk communication, and incorporating behavioral insights into security training programs. By understanding and addressing the psychological underpinnings of risk perception, organizations can develop more effective approaches to improving user compliance and overall security posture.

Leveraging insights from the psychology of risk perception can significantly enhance cybersecurity practices and policies. Effective security training programs can be designed to address common cognitive biases and emotional responses that influence behavior. For instance, incorporating real-world examples of cyber threats and providing practical, actionable advice can make training more engaging and impactful. Addressing how people emotionally react to potential risks helps users better recognize and respond to threats. Rather than focusing solely on technical details, training programs should also consider the psychological aspects of how individuals perceive and manage risk. This approach helps bridge the gap between theoretical knowledge and practical application, leading to improved security practices.

Similarly, enhancing risk communication involves crafting messages that resonate with the audience's perception of risk. By using a blend of factual information and relatable scenarios, organizations can make complex cybersecurity concepts more understandable and actionable. Illustrating threats through stories or real-life incidents can make the information more relatable and memorable, thus improving user engagement. Additionally, fostering a strong security culture within organizations is crucial. This includes addressing social norms and group dynamics by encouraging positive security behaviors, recognizing and rewarding compliance, and integrating cybersecurity into the organizational ethos. Creating an environment where secure practices are normalized and valued motivates individuals to adhere to best practices, contributing to a more resilient cybersecurity posture.

The psychology of risk perception plays a critical role in shaping cybersecurity behaviors and practices. By understanding the cognitive biases, emotional responses, and social influences that impact how individuals perceive and respond to cyber threats, we can develop more effective strategies for improving cybersecurity awareness and compliance. Addressing these psychological factors not only enhances individual security practices but also contributes to a more resilient overall security posture.

CHAPTER FOUR:
PHISHING AND SOCIAL ENGINEERING: EXPLOITING BEHAVIORAL VULNERABILITIES

Phishing and social engineering are prevalent and dangerous threats in the workings of cybersecurity. These tactics exploit human psychology rather than technological vulnerabilities, making them particularly insidious and effective. By understanding how phishing and social engineering manipulate behavioral vulnerabilities, we can better equip individuals and organizations to defend against these attacks. This chapter delves into the mechanisms behind these tactics, examines the psychological principles they exploit, and offers strategies for mitigation and prevention.

Understanding Phishing and Social Engineering

These concepts involve deceptive practices aimed at manipulating individuals into divulging sensitive information or performing actions that compromise security. Although they share similarities, they employ distinct methods and target different aspects of human behavior.

Phishing is a type of cyber-attack where attackers impersonate legitimate entities to trick individuals into providing confidential information, such as passwords or financial details. It typically occurs through email, but it can also be executed via text messages (smishing) or phone calls (vishing). Phishing attacks often use fake websites that resemble legitimate ones, making it difficult for users to distinguish between genuine and fraudulent communications. Social engineering encompasses a broader range of manipulative tactics designed to exploit psychological vulnerabilities. It involves manipulating individuals into performing actions or divulging information that they would not ordinarily share. Unlike phishing, which is often focused on stealing information, social engineering can involve a variety of deceptive techniques, such as pretexting, baiting, and tailgating.

These attacks rely on exploiting fundamental psychological principles to deceive their targets. Attackers often exploit the principle of authority by impersonating figures of authority or trusted organizations. For instance, an email appearing to come from an executive or a reputable company can create a sense of urgency or legitimacy, prompting individuals to act quickly without verifying the request. The authority principle plays on our inclination to trust and comply with perceived authoritative figures.

The scarcity principle involves creating a sense of urgency or limited availability to compel individuals to act quickly. Phishing emails often include statements like "Your account will be locked unless you act now" or "Limited-time offer" to induce panic and prompt hasty actions. This urgency can override rational decision-making processes, making individuals more susceptible to falling for the scam. The reciprocity principle leverages the natural human tendency to return favors or act in kind when someone has provided something. Social engineers may offer something of perceived value, such as a free download or a prize, to create a sense of obligation. Once individuals have accepted the initial offer, they may feel compelled to provide personal information or take actions that benefit the attacker.

Social proof involves using the behavior or endorsements of others to influence an individual's decisions. Phishing attacks may use social proof by including fake testimonials or references to peers who have supposedly taken similar actions. By suggesting that "everyone is doing it," attackers can create a false sense of consensus and legitimacy. Exploiting trust and familiarity is another common tactic. Attackers may impersonate known contacts or organizations, making their communications appear more credible. For instance, a phishing email might come from an address that closely resembles a trusted colleague's email, making it harder for recipients to recognize the fraudulent nature of the message.

They also employ a variety of techniques designed to deceive and manipulate targets. Some of the examples and methods are:

Email Phishing: This is one of the most common forms of phishing, where attackers send emails that appear to come from legitimate sources. These emails often contain malicious links or attachments designed to steal credentials or install malware. Examples include emails claiming to be from banks requesting account verification or from online services asking for password updates.

Spear Phishing: Unlike broad-based phishing, spear phishing targets specific individuals or organizations. Attackers gather detailed information about their targets, such as job roles or recent activities, to craft personalized and convincing messages. For example, an attacker might impersonate an HR department to request sensitive employee information, exploiting the recipient's trust and familiarity.

Pretexting: Pretexting involves creating a fabricated scenario to obtain information from the target. Attackers may pose as internal IT support or other legitimate figures and use this pretext to solicit personal or confidential information. For example, an attacker might call an employee pretending to be from the IT department and request login credentials for "verification purposes."

Baiting: Baiting involves offering something enticing to lure individuals into a trap. This could be in the form of a free software download, a promotional offer, or a physical item like a USB drive left in a public place. When individuals engage with the bait, they may inadvertently install malware or compromise their security.

Tailgating: This is a physical social engineering technique where an attacker gains unauthorized access to a secure area by following authorized personnel. For instance, an attacker might pose as a delivery person or maintenance worker and gain entry by following someone who swipes their access card.

Whaling: Whaling is a specialized form of spear phishing that targets high-profile individuals, such as executives or senior management, within an organization. Unlike generic phishing attacks, whaling involves highly personalized and often sophisticated approaches. Attackers gather detailed information about their targets, such as their role, recent business activities, or key relationships, to craft convincing and highly specific messages. For example, a whaling attack might involve an email that appears to come from a board member or major client, requesting sensitive financial information or urgent action on a high-stakes matter. The level of personalization and the apparent authority behind the message make whaling attacks particularly dangerous and difficult to detect.

Credential Stuffing: This involves using stolen or leaked username and password combinations to gain unauthorized access to accounts. Attackers use automated tools to try these credentials across multiple websites and services, taking advantage of individuals who reuse passwords. This technique is often preceded by phishing attacks that trick users into revealing their login details or by data breaches where credential information is obtained. For example, if a user's credentials are compromised through a phishing email, attackers might use those credentials to access their bank accounts, email, or other online services, potentially leading to further security breaches or financial losses.

Impersonation in Customer Service: Attackers may impersonate customer service representatives or support staff to deceive individuals into providing sensitive information or performing certain actions. This technique often involves crafting phone calls, emails, or live chat messages that appear to come from legitimate support channels. For instance, an attacker might call a user claiming to be from their internet service provider, informing them of a supposed issue with their account and requesting login credentials or other personal information for "verification purposes." By exploiting the trust individuals place in customer service interactions, attackers can bypass traditional security measures and gain access to valuable information or systems.

Impact and Consequences of Phishing and Social Engineering

The impact of phishing and social engineering attacks can be severe and far-reaching. These attacks not only compromise sensitive information but can also lead to significant financial and reputational damage for both individuals and organizations. When attackers successfully deceive victims, they can directly siphon funds through unauthorized transactions, fraud, or financial theft. For instance, a compromised bank account due to a phishing scam might result in substantial monetary loss as attackers drain funds or make fraudulent purchases. Beyond immediate financial impacts, organizations may also incur costs related to incident response, legal fees, and regulatory fines. The direct financial consequences can strain resources and disrupt normal operations, making effective prevention and response critical.

Additionally, phishing and social engineering attacks can have far-reaching effects on data security and organizational reputation. Data breaches resulting from these attacks often expose sensitive personal or corporate information, leading to identity theft, unauthorized use of information, and long-term financial repercussions for victims. The reputational damage to organizations can be severe, as trust in the company's security practices diminishes. This loss of customer confidence can result in reduced business opportunities, negative publicity, and long-lasting damage to the brand. Furthermore, operational disruptions caused by these attacks can lead to decreased productivity and operational inefficiencies, compounding the overall impact on an organization's effectiveness and profitability.

There are mechanisms that can be employed to mitigate and prevent the occurrences of these attacks. To effectively combat these attacks, organizations and individuals must implement a multi-layered approach to security. First, regular training and awareness programs are crucial for educating users about phishing and social engineering threats. Training should include practical examples, simulation exercises, and guidance on recognizing and reporting suspicious activities. By increasing awareness and vigilance, individuals are better equipped to identify and avoid potential attacks. Implementing MFA adds an extra layer of security by requiring multiple forms of verification before granting access. Even if attackers manage to obtain login credentials through phishing, MFA can prevent unauthorized access by requiring additional verification factors, such as a code sent to a mobile device.

Employing advanced email filtering solutions can help detect and block phishing attempts before they reach users. These solutions use various techniques, such as analyzing email content, checking sender reputations, and identifying suspicious patterns to filter out malicious messages. Establishing verification procedures for sensitive requests can help prevent social engineering attacks. For instance, implementing protocols for verifying requests for confidential information or financial transactions through secondary channels (e.g., phone calls or secure messaging) can reduce the risk of falling victim to impersonation attempts. Finally, developing and regularly updating an incident response plan is essential for effectively addressing phishing and social engineering attacks. The plan should include procedures for detecting, reporting, and mitigating attacks, as well as guidelines for communication and recovery. Regular drills and simulations can help ensure that the response plan is effective and that team members are prepared to act quickly in the event of an attack.

Phishing and social engineering exploit fundamental behavioral vulnerabilities to deceive and manipulate individuals. By understanding the psychological principles underlying these tactics and recognizing the various techniques used by attackers, individuals and organizations can better defend against these threats. Implementing comprehensive education and training programs, adopting advanced security measures, and establishing robust verification procedures are essential steps in mitigating the risks associated with phishing and social engineering. As the threat scope continues to evolve, staying informed and proactive in addressing these behavioral vulnerabilities will remain a critical component of an effective cybersecurity strategy.

CHAPTER FIVE:
THE INFLUENCE OF STRESS AND FATIGUE ON CYBERSECURITY PRACTICES

Human factors often overshadow technological defenses, with stress and fatigue emerging as significant contributors to security vulnerabilities. As the complexities in the internet becomes increasingly rampant, the interplay between psychological states and security practices has garnered attention. This chapter delves into how stress and fatigue influence cybersecurity behaviors, exploring their impact on decision-making, vulnerability management, and overall security posture. By understanding these psychological influences, we can develop more effective strategies to mitigate risks and enhance cybersecurity resilience.

Understanding Stress and Fatigue

Stress and fatigue are psychological and physiological states that can impair cognitive function and decision-making. Stress is a response to perceived threats or demands, triggering physiological and emotional reactions that can affect an individual's ability to perform tasks effectively. Fatigue, on the other hand, results from prolonged physical or mental exertion and can lead to diminished alertness and cognitive capacity.

Stress can arise from various sources, including workload pressures, organizational changes, or personal issues. In the context of cybersecurity, stress may stem from high-stakes security incidents, tight deadlines, or the constant need to stay updated with evolving threats. Stressful environments can lead to heightened anxiety, distraction, and impaired judgment, all of which can negatively impact cybersecurity practices. Fatigue is often a result of long hours, inadequate rest, or continuous engagement in mentally taxing activities. In cybersecurity, professionals may experience fatigue due to extended shifts, emergency response situations, or the monotonous nature of repetitive tasks. Fatigue impairs cognitive functions such as attention, memory, and decision-making, increasing the likelihood of errors and lapses in security practices.

Stress significantly affects cybersecurity practices by altering cognitive processes and decision-making abilities. Understanding these impacts can help in developing strategies to mitigate the adverse effects of stress. It can lead to cognitive overload, where the amount of information an individual needs to process exceeds their cognitive capacity. In case, this can manifest as difficulty in managing multiple tasks, analyzing complex threat data, or responding to security alerts. When overwhelmed, individuals are more likely to make errors, overlook critical details, or fail to follow established security protocols. Under high stress, decision-making processes may become impaired. Individuals may resort to heuristic-based decisions, which are quicker but often less accurate. For example, a stressed IT professional might prioritize resolving immediate issues without fully assessing the potential security risks involved. This can lead to hasty decisions that compromise security, such as applying incomplete patches or ignoring critical alerts.

It can also lead to increased risk-taking behavior, as individuals may become less cautious or more willing to take shortcuts to alleviate pressure. This could involve bypassing security protocols, using weak passwords, or neglecting routine security checks. The desire to quickly resolve a problem or meet a deadline may overshadow the need for thorough security practices. It can reduce individuals' capacity for maintaining vigilance and awareness of potential threats. Stressful situations may lead to a diminished ability to detect phishing attempts, recognize suspicious activities, or adhere to security best practices. Emotional responses such as frustration or anxiety can further cloud judgment and reduce overall security effectiveness.

Fatigue, resulting from prolonged or intense work periods, also has significant implications for cybersecurity practices. The effects of fatigue on cognitive function and behavior are crucial for understanding its impact on security. It impairs attention and vigilance, making it challenging for individuals to remain focused on security tasks. For example, a cybersecurity professional experiencing fatigue might struggle to monitor multiple security alerts or detect subtle signs of a security breach. This decreased attention can result in missed threats or delayed responses to critical issues. Fatigue affects memory and recall, which are essential for following security procedures and protocols. When fatigued, individuals may forget important steps in security processes, such as updating software, applying security patches, or following password policies. This can lead to lapses in security practices and increased susceptibility to cyber threats.

It leads to an increased error rate and overall performance degradation. Repetitive tasks, such as monitoring logs or performing routine security checks, can become more prone to mistakes when individuals are tired. Errors in these tasks can have serious consequences, including missed vulnerabilities or overlooked security incidents. It negatively impacts decision-making quality, resulting in less effective responses to security challenges. Individuals may struggle to analyze complex security data, prioritize tasks effectively, or make informed decisions under pressure. This can lead to suboptimal security measures and increased risk exposure.

Organizational and Environmental Factors Contributing to Stress and Fatigue

Understanding the organizational and environmental factors that contribute to stress and fatigue is essential for addressing their impact on cybersecurity practices.

Workload and Job Demands: High workload and job demands can contribute significantly to stress and fatigue among cybersecurity professionals. Extended work hours, tight deadlines, and the constant need to address security threats can lead to burnout and diminished performance. Organizations must manage workloads and ensure that employees have adequate time to rest and recover.

Support and Resources: Lack of support and resources can exacerbate stress and fatigue. Inadequate training, limited access to tools, or insufficient staffing can increase the burden on cybersecurity professionals, leading to heightened stress levels and fatigue. Providing adequate support, resources, and training is crucial for maintaining effective cybersecurity practices.

Work Environment and Culture: The work environment and organizational culture play a role in influencing stress and fatigue levels. A high-pressure or toxic work culture can increase stress, while a supportive and collaborative environment can mitigate its effects. Organizations should foster a positive work culture that promotes well-being and supports employees in managing stress and fatigue.

Emergency Response Situations: During security incidents or emergency response situations, stress and fatigue can be particularly acute. The urgency and high stakes of such situations can lead to heightened stress and prolonged periods of intense focus. Implementing strategies to manage emergency response effectively and providing support during and after such events is crucial for maintaining security performance.

Implementing strategies to manage and mitigate these factors can enhance overall security effectiveness.

Addressing stress and fatigue in cybersecurity requires a comprehensive approach that includes promoting work-life balance and providing adequate training and resources. Encouraging a healthy work-life balance is fundamental; organizations should support flexible work schedules and discourage excessive overtime to prevent burnout. Providing employees with time for rest and recovery is crucial for maintaining their effectiveness and well-being. Additionally, offering training programs focused on stress management, effective time management, and productivity techniques can equip individuals with the skills needed to handle pressure more effectively. Access to resources such as mental health support, ergonomic workstations, and wellness programs further contributes to reducing stress and fatigue. By fostering an environment where employees are encouraged to manage their workload and seek support when needed, organizations can mitigate the negative impacts of stress and fatigue on security practices.

Optimizing work processes and tools also plays a key role in managing stress and fatigue. Streamlining workflows, automating repetitive tasks, and improving the usability of security tools can alleviate cognitive load and reduce the mental strain associated with complex security tasks. Regularly monitoring and managing workload to prevent excessive demands is essential, as is redistributing tasks and providing additional support during peak periods. Building robust support systems, including counseling services and peer support networks, can help employees cope with challenging situations and maintain their well-being. Leadership's role in promoting a supportive culture and leading by example is also critical; leaders should advocate for well-being initiatives and demonstrate a commitment to managing stress and fatigue. By implementing these strategies, organizations can enhance their cybersecurity effectiveness and create a healthier work environment for their teams.

The Role of Leadership in Addressing Stress and Fatigue

Leadership plays a critical role in managing stress and fatigue within cybersecurity teams. Effective leadership can influence organizational culture, support systems, and overall well-being. Leaders which could be managers, team leads, heads of department and top executives can integrate some of these practices to ensure the moderation of stress and fatigue among their teams.

Promoting a Supportive Culture: Leaders should foster a supportive culture that prioritizes employee well-being and recognizes the impact of stress and fatigue. Encouraging open dialogue, providing regular feedback, and acknowledging the challenges faced by cybersecurity professionals can help create a positive work environment.

Leading by Example: Leaders should model healthy work behaviors and demonstrate a commitment to managing stress and fatigue. By setting an example and prioritizing their own well-being, leaders can influence the organizational culture and encourage employees to adopt similar practices.

Implementing Well-Being Initiatives: They should champion well-being initiatives and ensure that resources and support systems are available to employees. This includes advocating for mental health support, wellness programs, and work-life balance initiatives. Leadership involvement in these initiatives can enhance their effectiveness and demonstrate a commitment to employee well-being.

Stress and fatigue significantly impact cybersecurity practices, influencing decision-making, attention, and overall performance. By understanding the psychological effects of these factors and implementing strategies to manage them, organizations can enhance their cybersecurity posture and reduce vulnerabilities. Addressing stress and fatigue through work-life balance initiatives, support systems, optimized work processes, and effective leadership is essential for maintaining a resilient and effective security workforce. To achieve the best possible outcomes, prioritizing the well-being of cybersecurity professionals will remain a crucial component of a robust and secure security strategy.

CHAPTER SIX:
USER AWARENESS AND TRAINING: BRIDGING THE GAP BETWEEN KNOWLEDGE AND ACTION

The human element often represents the weakest link when dealing with security in digital infrastructure settings. Despite the implementation of sophisticated security measures and advanced technologies, many organizations find that their greatest vulnerabilities lie in user behavior. In this chapter, we will learn the importance of user awareness and training, exploring how to effectively bridge the gap between knowledge and action, and provides practical strategies for organizations to implement comprehensive user awareness and training programs.

What is the Human Factor in Cybersecurity

Human behavior is a critical factor in cybersecurity. Studies consistently show that human error is a leading cause of security breaches. Phishing attacks, weak password practices, and improper handling of sensitive information are all examples where human actions can compromise security. The challenge lies not just in recognizing these behaviors but in changing them.

Knowledge alone does not guarantee safe behavior. Many users understand the risks associated with cyber threats but fail to act accordingly due to a variety of reasons including forgetfulness, lack of motivation, or simply not understanding the practical application of their knowledge. Bridging the gap between understanding these security principles and applying them effectively requires a more nuanced approach that combines education with practical, actionable training.

The next pertinent question is the importance of user awareness and training. There are several that can be attributed to implementing this mechanism effectively. One, they are essential components of a robust security strategy. By educating individuals on potential threats and the best practices for mitigating them, organizations can significantly reduce their risk of incidents. Proper training helps users recognize phishing attempts, avoid malware infections, and follow secure practices, ultimately contributing to a more secure overall environment. They are also often mandated by regulations and compliance standards. Many frameworks, such as GDPR, HIPAA, and PCI-DSS, require organizations to implement regular training programs for employees to ensure they understand their responsibilities and adhere to best practices. Non-compliance can result in significant fines and legal consequences, making it crucial for organizations to invest in effective training programs.

They play a crucial role in enhancing organizational resilience. When employees are well-versed in cybersecurity best practices, they become more adept at identifying and responding to potential threats. This increased vigilance helps to minimize the impact of security incidents by ensuring that users can recognize and react appropriately to suspicious activities, thereby preventing minor issues from escalating into major breaches. A workforce that understands the nuances of cybersecurity can contribute to quicker detection and response times, ultimately reducing downtime and maintaining business continuity during and after an incident. This proactive approach not only safeguards sensitive information but also supports the overall stability and robustness of the organization's operations.

Effective user awareness and training foster a culture of security within a workplace. When employees are continuously educated about the importance of security and their role in protecting the organization's assets, they are more likely to adopt secure behaviors and practices. This cultural shift promotes a collective responsibility, where everyone from the top executives to entry-level staff members is invested in maintaining a secure environment. By embedding awareness into the organizational culture, companies can create an environment where security considerations are integrated into everyday decision-making processes, leading to more informed and cautious behavior across the board. This cultural emphasis helps in cultivating a strong defense against cyber threats and ensures that security is not just a top-down mandate but a shared value embraced by all members of the organization.

Designing Effective User Awareness and Training Programs

This section will cover a guide on how to design awareness and training programs that are effective and beneficial to an organization. There are several steps to take namely:

Assessing Training Needs

Before developing a training program, it is essential to assess the specific needs of the organization and its employees. This involves identifying common security threats relevant to the organization's industry, evaluating existing knowledge gaps, and understanding the specific challenges users face. Surveys, interviews, and security incident analysis can provide valuable insights into these needs.

Developing Training Content

Effective training content should be engaging, relevant, and tailored to the audience. It should cover key topics such as:

Phishing Awareness: Teaching users how to recognize phishing emails, avoid clicking on suspicious links, and verify the legitimacy of requests for sensitive information.

Password Management: Educating persons on the importance of strong passwords, the use of password managers, and the dangers of password reuse.

Data Protection: Providing guidelines on handling sensitive data, including encryption, secure file sharing, and proper disposal of confidential information.

Safe Internet Practices: Offering advice on secure browsing, avoiding suspicious websites, and understanding the risks of downloading files from untrusted sources.

Incident Reporting: Instructing users on how to report suspicious activities and potential security incidents promptly.

Choosing the Right Training Methods

Different training methods can be used to deliver content effectively. These include:

Online Training Modules: Interactive e-learning courses that persons can complete at their own pace. These modules can include quizzes, simulations, and scenario-based exercises to reinforce learning.

In-Person Workshops: Hands-on sessions led by cybersecurity experts where individuals can engage in discussions, ask questions, and participate in practical exercises.

Simulated Attacks: Conducting simulated phishing attacks or social engineering exercises to test users' responses and provide real-time feedback.

Regular Updates and Refresher Courses: Providing ongoing training to keep users informed about the latest threats and best practices.

Measuring Effectiveness

To ensure that the training program is effective, organizations should regularly evaluate its impact. Key performance indicators (KPIs) might include:

Completion Rates: Tracking how many employees complete the training modules.

Knowledge Retention: Assessing users' understanding of key concepts through quizzes or assessments before and after training.

Behavioral Changes: Monitoring changes in user behavior, such as a reduction in the number of security incidents or phishing attempts reported.

Feedback and Surveys: Gathering feedback from individuals about the training experience and identifying areas for improvement.

Practical Implementation of User Awareness and Training Programs

A Step-by-Step Guide

1. Establish Objectives: Define clear goals for the training program, such as improving phishing detection rates or enhancing password management practices.

2. Develop a Training Plan: Outline the content to be covered, the methods of delivery, and the schedule for training sessions. Include both initial training and ongoing education.

3. Create or Source Content: Develop training materials or partner with external vendors to provide relevant content. Ensure that the material is up-to-date and aligned with current threats and best practices.

4. Implement Training: Roll out the training program to employees. Utilize a mix of delivery methods to cater to different learning styles and ensure broad engagement.

5. Evaluate and Adapt: Continuously assess the effectiveness of the training program through surveys, incident tracking, and performance metrics. Use this information to make necessary adjustments and improvements.

Overcoming Common Challenges

Organizations may face several challenges when implementing user awareness and training programs. Addressing these challenges proactively can enhance the effectiveness of the program.

For instance, ensuring that the training is engaging and relevant helps to avoid user disengagement. By incorporating interactive elements and real-world scenarios, the content can be made more relatable. Balancing the need for comprehensive training with budget limitations is also imperative. Consider cost-effective methods such as online modules or in-house training. Tailoring training content to accommodate diverse audiences and addressing language barriers to ensure that all users can benefit from the training can be an effective tactic. It is also beneficial to regularly update training materials to reflect the latest threats and technological advancements. Endeavour to establish a process for ongoing content review and revision.

Case Studies and Success Stories

Case Study 1: Financial Services Firm

A large financial services firm implemented a comprehensive user awareness and training program in response to a series of phishing attacks that had compromised several employee accounts. The program included interactive e-learning modules, simulated phishing attacks, and regular workshops. Within six months, the firm observed a significant decrease in successful phishing attempts and improved incident reporting rates. Employee feedback indicated that the training was engaging and valuable, and the firm reported enhanced overall security posture.

Case Study 2: Healthcare Provider

A healthcare provider faced challenges with ensuring compliance with HIPAA regulations and protecting sensitive patient information. The organization introduced a targeted training program focusing on data protection, password management, and incident reporting. The program included role-based training to address specific responsibilities and risks for different departments. As a result, the provider saw a marked improvement in data handling practices, fewer compliance violations, and increased confidence among employees in managing sensitive information.

User awareness and training are critical components of a comprehensive cybersecurity strategy. By bridging the gap between knowledge and action, organizations can empower their employees to act as the first line of defense against cyber threats. Effective training programs that address specific needs, employ diverse delivery methods, and incorporate practical, actionable content can significantly enhance an organization's security posture.

CHAPTER SEVEN:
THE ROLE OF ORGANIZATIONAL CULTURE IN SHAPING SECURITY BEHAVIOR

It is no news that cybersecurity has become a critical concern for organizations worldwide. While technological solutions are essential for protecting sensitive information, the human element remains a significant factor in security as earlier stated across this book. One crucial aspect of the human element is organizational culture, which profoundly influences security behavior within a company. Organizational culture encompasses the values, beliefs, and norms that guide employee behavior and decision-making. Understanding how culture affects security behavior is vital for developing effective security strategies and fostering a security-conscious environment.

Organizational Culture: An overview

Organizational culture refers to the collective values, beliefs, and behaviors that shape how work gets done within an organization. It is reflected in the organization's practices, traditions, and day-to-day operations. Key elements of organizational culture include values, beliefs, norms, and rituals. Values refer to core beliefs that guide decisions and actions while beliefs are assumptions about how the world works and how it should work. Norms are unwritten rules and expectations that govern behavior and rituals are regular practices and ceremonies that reinforce the culture.

Culture is shaped by various factors, including leadership, history, and industry norms. It is communicated through both formal channels (e.g., mission statements, policies) and informal ones (e.g., social interactions, storytelling). Different institutions may have varying cultures, such as hierarchical (emphasizing structure and control), innovative (encouraging creativity and risk-taking), or collaborative (focusing on teamwork and mutual support).

Company culture plays a crucial role in shaping employees' attitudes toward security. In organizations where security is a high priority, employees are more likely to view these practices as integral to their roles. For instance, a firm that consistently emphasizes the importance of data protection and invests in security training is likely to foster a culture where employees are vigilant and proactive about cybersecurity. Conversely, in organizations where security is seen as a low priority or an obstacle to productivity, employees may be less inclined to adhere to set protocols. This can lead to risky behaviors, such as bypassing protection measures or neglecting to follow best practices. The leadership's role is pivotal in setting the tone for security culture. Leaders who model security-conscious behavior and communicate its importance effectively can positively influence employees' attitudes and behaviors.

Cultural norms also impact how employees comply with security policies. In a strong security culture, adherence to policies is seen as part of the organization's values and expectations. Employees are more likely to follow procedures when they perceive them as integral to the institution's mission and their role within it. Peer behavior and informal social controls also play a role. In a culture where security is valued, employees are more likely to hold each other accountable and reinforce practices among their peers. In contrast, in a culture where security is not emphasized, compliance may be inconsistent. Employees may prioritize convenience over security, leading to behaviors such as using weak passwords or ignoring security updates. Peer pressure and the lack of a collective commitment to these mechanisms can exacerbate these issues, making it essential for organizations to cultivate a culture where security is a shared responsibility.

Effective communication and training are critical components of a security culture. Cultural factors influence how well these training programs are received and implemented. In firms with a collaborative environment, training is often seen as a shared responsibility, and employees are more likely to engage with and apply what they learn. Conversely, in hierarchical cultures, training may be perceived as a top-down directive, which can impact its effectiveness. The style and frequency of communication about security also matter. In a culture that values transparency and open communication, security policies and updates are regularly discussed, and employees feel comfortable asking questions and seeking clarification. In contrast, in cultures where communication is less open, employees may be less informed about security issues and less motivated to adhere to policies.

Several organizations have successfully fostered a strong culture, leading to improved security behaviors and outcomes. For example, companies like Google and

Microsoft have implemented comprehensive programs that emphasize the importance of security at all levels. These firms use a combination of leadership commitment, regular training, and clear communication to reinforce security practices. Google's approach includes integrating security into its core values and ensuring that it is a shared responsibility across teams. This approach has contributed to a culture where security is taken seriously, and employees actively contribute to protecting the organization's assets.

On the other hand, there are cases where cultural factors have led to significant security breaches. One notable example is the 2013 Target data breach, which exposed the personal information of millions of customers. Investigations revealed that cultural issues, such as a lack of emphasis on security at the executive level and inadequate communication between departments, played a role in the breach. The company's culture did not prioritize security as a core value, leading to insufficient protection measures and a failure to address known vulnerabilities. These examples highlight the importance of aligning organizational culture with security objectives. Institutions that prioritize security and integrate it into their culture are better positioned to protect themselves from threats and respond effectively to incidents.

Assessing and Shaping Security Culture

To understand how culture affects security behavior, organizations must assess their current stance. This involves evaluating employees' attitudes toward security, their adherence to policies, and the effectiveness of communication and training programs. Tools such as surveys, focus groups, and interviews can provide valuable insights into cultural factors influencing security behavior. Surveys can assess employees' perceptions of security policies, their understanding of the risks, and their willingness to follow best practices. Focus groups and interviews can provide qualitative insights into the cultural factors that impact security behavior, such as leadership attitudes and peer influences. Regular assessments can help organizations identify areas for improvement and track progress over time.

Once an institution understands its current security position, it can take steps to shape and improve it. To effectively shape and improve security culture within an organization, several key strategies should be employed. Leadership commitment is paramount; leaders should actively model security-conscious behavior and consistently communicate the importance of security. Their dedication can set a positive example for the entire company, embedding the concept into the organizational ethos and reinforcing it as a core value. Alongside this, integrating it into a body value system ensures that security practices are aligned with the company's broader goals. By emphasizing the role of each individual in achieving these goals, organizations can create a unified approach where security is perceived as integral to overall success rather than an isolated concern.

Additionally, engaging persons in the development and implementation of protection policies is crucial for fostering a security-conscious culture. When employees are involved in discussions about security, they are more likely to buy into the policies and adhere to them. To support this, providing ongoing training is essential. Regular updates on security best practices help maintain awareness and reinforce the importance of security. Training programs should be tailored to the organization's specific culture, addressing relevant risks and challenges to ensure they are practical and effective in reinforcing security practices across the organization.

There are challenges that can be encountered in the process and some considerations that can be undertaken to resolve them.

Resistance to Change: Changing organizational culture can be challenging, especially if there is resistance from employees or leadership. Common obstacles include entrenched attitudes, lack of motivation, and conflicting priorities. Overcoming resistance requires a strategic approach, including clear communication, addressing concerns, and demonstrating the benefits of cultural change.

Balancing Security and Innovation: Organizations must balance stringent security measures with the need for innovation and flexibility. A security culture that is too rigid may stifle creativity and hinder productivity. Finding the right balance involves implementing protection measures that protect assets without unduly impeding operations. Organizations should focus on creating a culture where security and innovation can coexist, ensuring that security practices support rather than hinder institutional goals.

Cultural Misalignment Across Global Offices: For multinational companies, aligning security culture across diverse global offices can be particularly challenging. Different regions may have distinct cultural norms, attitudes, and regulatory requirements that impact how these policies are perceived and implemented. For instance, what is considered a standard practice in one country might be seen as excessive or impractical in another country. This cultural misalignment can lead to inconsistent measures or practices and gaps in protection. To address this, organizations need to develop a flexible security framework that can be adapted to local contexts while maintaining core security principles. Effective communication and localized training programs are essential to bridge cultural differences and ensure that these policies are uniformly understood and followed across all offices.

Evolving Threat Landscape: The rapidly changing trends in threat presents another significant challenge in shaping security culture. As new cyber threats and attack vectors emerge, organizations must continuously update their security practices and training programs to address these changes. However, keeping pace with evolving threats can be difficult, particularly if the firm's culture is not adaptable or responsive to change. A culture that resists or is slow to adopt new security measures can leave the organization vulnerable to attacks. To mitigate this challenge, companies should foster a culture of agility and continuous learning. This includes encouraging employees to stay informed about the latest threats and incorporating regular updates into training programs. By promoting a proactive and adaptable approach to security, they can better respond to emerging threats and maintain a strong security posture.

As technology and work environments evolve, so too will the role of organizational culture in shaping security behavior. One notable trend is the rise of remote work, which introduces new challenges and opportunities for cultivating a robust security culture. Organizations will need to adapt their security practices to address the unique risks associated with remote work, ensuring that employees are equipped with the right tools and knowledge to maintain protection outside the traditional office setting. Also, the ongoing digital transformation, characterized by an increasing reliance on digital tools and platforms, necessitates a continuous evolution of security culture. Emphasizing the importance of security within the context of digital transformation will be crucial for companies to sustain a strong security posture and effectively manage emerging threats.

Organizational culture plays a critical role in shaping security behavior and influencing how employees approach cybersecurity. By understanding the impact of culture on these practices, institutions can develop strategies to foster a security-conscious environment and mitigate risks. Leadership commitment, effective communication, and ongoing training are key components to bear in mind while developing a strong culture.

CHAPTER EIGHT:
BEHAVIORAL ECONOMICS IN CYBERSECURITY

The need to understand human behavior has been extensively discussed as a crucial activity in cybersecurity. Security threats are increasingly sophisticated, and human error remains a significant vulnerability. Behavioral economics, a field that blends insights from psychology and economics, provides a framework to understand how individuals make decisions, particularly in contexts involving risk and uncertainty. We will explore how principles of behavioral economics can be applied to enhance security practices, focusing on incentives, penalties, and decision-making.

The Basics of Behavioral Economics

Behavioral economics challenges the traditional economic assumption that individuals are perfectly rational agents who always make decisions that maximize their utility. Instead, it posits that humans often exhibit systematic biases and cognitive errors.

Key concepts in behavioral economics that are particularly relevant to cybersecurity include heuristics and biases, prospect theory, and nudging. Heuristics and biases refer to mental shortcuts or "rules of thumb" that simplify decision-making but can also lead to predictable errors. For example, the availability heuristic might cause individuals to overestimate the likelihood of security threats based on recent or memorable incidents, potentially leading to an overemphasis on certain risks while neglecting others. Prospect theory, another important concept, suggests that people value gains and losses differently, with losses typically having a greater emotional impact than equivalent gains. This can influence how individuals perceive and react to potential security threats, often making the fear of loss a stronger motivator than the potential for gain. Finally, nudging involves subtly guiding individuals toward better decisions without restricting their freedom of choice. In this context, nudges can be employed to encourage safer practices such as setting strong passwords or enabling multi-factor authentication by making these options more convenient or salient, rather than relying on strict mandates or punitive measures.

Incentives play a crucial role in shaping behaviors and ensuring compliance with security protocols. Positive incentives, such as recognition and rewards, are effective tools for encouraging employees to adhere to best practices. For example, organizations might implement a system where employees receive praise, bonuses, or other forms of acknowledgment for consistently following procedures, such as using strong passwords or reporting suspicious emails. This not only motivates individuals to prioritize security but also reinforces the importance of safe behaviors within the company.

On the other hand, negative incentives involve penalties or consequences for failing to adhere to protocols. Financial penalties or formal reprimands can serve as deterrents to risky behaviors and non-compliance. For instance, an organization might impose fines or issue warnings for repeated breaches of data protection policies. Additionally, increasing scrutiny and monitoring of employees who consistently fail to comply with measures can further deter non-compliance. However, it is crucial that such penalties are perceived as fair and are consistently enforced to avoid fostering resentment or resistance among employees.

A balanced approach that combines both positive and negative incentives is often most effective. For example, a program that rewards compliance while also implementing consequences for non-compliance can create a robust culture of security. By acknowledging and rewarding safe practices, institutions can reinforce the desired behaviors, while penalties serve as a reminder of the importance of adherence to protocols. Nonetheless, it is essential to design incentives carefully to avoid unintended consequences, such as employees circumventing measures to avoid penalties or feeling demotivated by perceived unfairness. Ultimately, the effectiveness of incentives hinges on their thoughtful implementation and alignment with organizational goals. They should be designed to encourage secure behaviors, foster a positive culture, and support the overall objectives of the organization's strategy.

Penalties can influence behavior significantly, but their effectiveness is influenced by several factors, including perceived fairness and the likelihood of enforcement. One critical aspect is perceived fairness; penalties are more effective when they are seen as fair and transparent. If employees believe that they are applied consistently and equitably, they are more likely to comply with protocols. For example, if the rules regarding data breaches are clear and uniformly enforced, employees are more likely to follow them. Conversely, perceived unfairness can lead to resistance, decreased morale, and even attempts to bypass rules.

The likelihood of enforcement also plays a crucial role in the effectiveness of penalties. Employees are more likely to adhere to protocols if they believe there is a high probability of detection and consequences. This means that organizations must ensure robust monitoring systems are in place and that penalties are consistently enforced. For instance, if employees are aware that breaches will be detected and penalized, they are more likely to follow security measures diligently. However, there is a risk of over-penalization, where excessively harsh or frequent penalties may have negative effects. Such measures can lead to decreased job satisfaction, a reduction in trust toward management, and attempts to circumvent rules. It is important to strike a balance where deterrents are effective without creating a hostile work environment. Careful consideration should be given to the design and application of punishment to ensure they reinforce rather than undermine the desired behaviors.

The successful application of penalties depends on their perceived fairness, the likelihood of enforcement, and their impact on organizational culture. Ensuring that penalties are fair and applied consistently, combined with appropriate monitoring and support, helps in maintaining compliance and fostering a positive environment.

Decision-Making and Cybersecurity

Understanding how individuals make decisions can help organizations design more effective security strategies. Several behavioral economics concepts are particularly relevant:

Risk Perception: Individuals' perception of risk influences their behavior. People often underestimate the probability of negative events occurring to them, a bias known as the optimism bias. In this setting, this can lead to complacency. To counteract this, organizations can use data and simulations to demonstrate the real risks and potential impacts of security threats.

Loss Aversion: According to prospect theory, people are more motivated to avoid losses than to achieve equivalent gains. This principle can be leveraged in cybersecurity by framing security practices in terms of avoiding losses rather than achieving gains. For example, emphasizing the potential loss of sensitive data or the impact of a security breach can be more motivating than highlighting the benefits of strong security.

Social Norms: People often look to others for cues on how to behave. By establishing and promoting strong security norms within an organization, companies can leverage social influence to encourage adherence to best practices. This can include leadership modeling secure behaviors and fostering a culture where security is a shared responsibility.

Behavioral Nudges: Nudges can be used to guide individuals toward better security practices without restricting their freedom. Examples include setting secure configurations as the default option, such as requiring multi-factor authentication, can nudge users to adopt these practices without requiring active decision-making. Making security procedures simple and straightforward can reduce the cognitive load on persons, making it easier for them to comply with security measures.

User education is essential for effective cybersecurity, yet traditional approaches often fall short due to the complexities of human behavior. Insights from behavioral economics can significantly enhance how security training is delivered, making it more engaging and impactful. One key application is tailoring training to address cognitive biases that affect how humans perceive and respond to information. For instance, users often rely on mental shortcuts, such as the availability heuristic, which leads them to overestimate the likelihood of recent threats and overlook less obvious risks. Training programs can leverage this by using recent, relatable examples of security breaches to make potential threats more memorable. Additionally, users tend to underestimate their vulnerability due to optimism bias, so training should present real-world statistics and personalized risk assessments to emphasize the actual probability of threats.

Gamification is another powerful tool that incorporates game-like elements into training to boost engagement and motivation. By introducing point systems, leaderboards, and interactive scenarios, organizations can make learning more dynamic and enjoyable. For example, users might earn points for successfully identifying phishing attempts in simulations, with top performers recognized on a leaderboard. This not only adds a competitive element but also fosters a sense of achievement. Interactive scenarios allow users to practice responding to security threats in a controlled environment, helping them learn from mistakes in a safe setting. Nudging is another principle that can be applied to guide users toward better security practices without limiting their choices. Simple strategies such as setting secure configurations as defaults, providing regular reminders and prompts, and using visual cues and feedback can nudge persons towards safer behaviors. For instance, automatically enabling multi-factor authentication and requiring strong passwords can significantly reduce the risk of security breaches. Regular prompts to update passwords or alerts about new security policies can also help maintain a focus on security.

Social influence plays a significant role in shaping behavior, and leveraging it can enhance the effectiveness of this training. Highlighting the security practices of respected peers or leaders can encourage others to follow suit, while demonstrating that a majority of users adhere to these protocols can create a sense of normativity around good practices. For example, showcasing how high-performing employees consistently follow security best practices can set a positive example for others. Personalization and relevance are crucial for effective training. Tailoring content to specific roles or departments ensures that the training addresses the unique risks and responsibilities of different user groups. Contextualized learning, which integrates training into users' daily workflows and provides relevant scenarios, makes the training experience more practical and applicable. For instance, embedding security tips within commonly used applications can reinforce good practices in a relevant context. Finally, measuring and adapting training programs based on user engagement and performance data is essential for maintaining their effectiveness. Tracking completion rates, test scores, and feedback provides valuable insights into the program's impact and areas for improvement. Continuous refinement based on this data ensures that the training remains relevant and engaging, adapting to emerging threats and evolving user needs.

Effective security strategies must be tailored to the unique characteristics and motivations of different individuals and groups. For example, technical staff may respond better to different incentives compared to non-technical employees. To ensure interventions are impactful, it is essential to regularly evaluate their effectiveness and seek feedback from employees. This continuous improvement approach helps companies adapt to changing threats and needs. Moreover, fostering a strong security culture is vital for long-term success. This involves creating an environment where this awareness is integrated into daily practices and viewed as a shared responsibility.

Behavioral economics offers valuable insights into how individuals make decisions and respond to incentives and penalties. By applying these principles, organizations can design more effective strategies to promote secure behaviors and mitigate risks. Balancing incentives, understanding behavioral biases, and fostering a strong security culture are crucial for enhancing security practices and protecting against evolving threats.

CHAPTER NINE:
DESIGNING USER-FRIENDLY SECURITY SOLUTIONS

Security solutions must be robust enough to defend against threats while also being user-friendly to ensure widespread adoption and compliance. When security measures are too complex or cumbersome, users might bypass them, inadvertently creating vulnerabilities. Conversely, overly simplified security solutions might not provide adequate protection. This chapter explores the strategies and considerations involved in designing user-friendly security solutions that effectively balance usability with protection, ensuring that security measures are both effective and accessible.

The Importance of Usability in Security

User-friendly security solutions are essential for several reasons. Primarily, usability impacts the likelihood of persons following security protocols. Complex or cumbersome protection measures often lead to user frustration and non-compliance, thereby reducing the overall effectiveness of security systems. For instance, if a multi-factor authentication (MFA) system is perceived as too complicated, users may opt to disable it or use weaker passwords instead. Moreover, a focus on usability helps in integrating security measures seamlessly into users' daily routines. When security protocols are intuitive and fit naturally within existing workflows, individuals are less likely to view them as obstacles and more likely to adopt them as standard practices. For example, implementing a password manager that integrates smoothly with browsers and applications can help users manage their passwords securely without significant disruption to their work.

Designing security solutions with usability in mind involves several key principles and practices. These principles ensure that security measures are both effective and easy to use.

Simplicity and Clarity: Simplicity is fundamental in designing user-friendly security solutions. Security features should be straightforward and easy to understand. Complex configurations or ambiguous instructions can lead to errors and reduce compliance. For instance, a user-friendly login process should minimize the number of steps required and clearly communicate any necessary actions, such as password resets or MFA prompts. To achieve clarity, designers should use plain language and intuitive design elements. Visual cues, such as clear icons and straightforward instructions, help persons navigate security features more effectively. For example, a well-designed password strength indicator provides immediate feedback on password choices, guiding users to create stronger passwords without requiring deep technical knowledge.

Minimizing User Effort: Reducing the effort required from individuals enhances the usability of security solutions. When security measures demand excessive input or frequent actions, users may become frustrated or disengaged. For example, solutions that require users to remember and enter multiple passwords for different services can be cumbersome and lead to poor password practices. To minimize user effort, designers can implement single sign-on (SSO) solutions that allow users to access multiple systems with a single set of credentials. Additionally, automating routine security tasks, such as password changes and software updates, can reduce the burden on users and ensure that security measures are consistently applied.

Providing Feedback and Guidance: Effective feedback and guidance are crucial for usability. Users should receive immediate and clear feedback when interacting with security features. For instance, if a person enters an incorrect password, they should receive a specific and helpful error message that guides them on how to correct the issue. Guidance should be proactive, offering users support and tips throughout their interaction with security measures. For example, onboarding tutorials or context-sensitive help can assist individuals in understanding and configuring security settings. This approach not only improves usability but also enhances overall security by ensuring that users are aware of and can effectively use security features.

Designing for Diverse User Needs: These solutions must account for the diverse needs and capabilities of users. Different individuals may have varying levels of technical expertise and accessibility requirements, making it important to design solutions that accommodate these differences. For instance, a security solution should be accessible to users with disabilities. This includes designing interfaces that are compatible with screen readers and providing alternative input methods for users with motor impairments. Additionally, security solutions should offer customization options to accommodate varying levels of technical expertise. For example, advanced settings might be hidden by default but made accessible for users who need them.

Balancing Protection and Usability

Achieving a balance between protection and usability involves addressing potential trade-offs and finding solutions that provide adequate security without compromising user experience.

A risk-based approach helps in balancing protection and usability by evaluating the level of risk associated with different user actions and adjusting security measures accordingly. For example, a high-risk action, such as accessing sensitive data, might require more stringent authentication measures, while lower-risk actions might involve less intrusive security checks. By tailoring security measures to the risk level, organizations can implement more rigorous protections where they are most needed while maintaining a more seamless experience for less critical tasks. This approach ensures that users are not burdened with excessive security measures for low-risk activities, improving overall usability.

Adaptive security measures adjust the level of protection based on contextual factors such as user behavior, location, and device. For example, if a person accesses an application from an unfamiliar device or location, additional authentication steps might be required. Conversely, familiar and secure environments might allow for more streamlined access. This helps maintain a balance between usability and protection by providing stronger safeguards when necessary while allowing for a more user-friendly experience under normal conditions. This dynamic approach ensures that security measures are appropriate for the context in which they are used.

Educating users about the importance of security and how to effectively use security features is crucial for balancing protection and usability. Effective training and awareness programs help individuals understand why certain measures are in place and how they contribute to overall security. For example, providing clear explanations about the purpose of MFA and demonstrating how to use it can help users appreciate the added security and reduce resistance to its implementation. Additionally, regular reminders and updates about security best practices can reinforce the importance of following security protocols.

Examining real-world implementations can offer valuable insights into achieving a balance between usability and protection in security solutions. One notable example is password managers, which epitomize a user-friendly approach to security. These tools are designed to securely store and manage passwords, simplifying the process for individuals while promoting the use of complex and unique passwords for different accounts. By automating password entry and offering features such as password generation and autofill, password managers alleviate the cognitive burden on users, reducing the risk of password fatigue and improving overall security.

Another pertinent example is the evolution of Multi-Factor Authentication (MFA). Traditional MFA methods, which often involved entering codes received via SMS or email, could be cumbersome and disrupt user workflows. Modern MFA solutions have improved usability significantly through advancements such as biometric authentication, which uses fingerprints or facial recognition, and push notifications, which deliver authentication requests directly to users' devices. These innovations make the MFA process more seamless and less intrusive, enhancing both convenience and security.

Single Sign-On (SSO) solutions further illustrate the balance between usability and protection. SSO systems allow users to access multiple applications and systems with a single set of credentials, reducing the number of passwords they need to remember. This simplification helps mitigate password fatigue and promotes the use of stronger passwords. Additionally, SSO solutions integrate smoothly into users' workflows, providing a more streamlined and efficient experience while maintaining centralized control over access, thus bolstering overall security.

Despite advancements, designing user-friendly security solutions presents ongoing challenges. Balancing usability with protection requires continuous innovation and adaptation to emerging threats and user needs. Some of these issues include:

Addressing Usability Issues: One challenge is addressing usability issues that arise from evolving security threats. As cyber threats become more sophisticated, security measures may need to become more complex, potentially impacting usability. Designers must find ways to incorporate advanced security features while maintaining a user-friendly experience.

Emerging Technologies: These technologies, such as artificial intelligence and machine learning, offer new opportunities for enhancing security solutions. These technologies can provide adaptive and context-aware security measures that balance protection and usability. For example, AI-powered threat detection systems can analyze user behavior to identify potential risks and adjust security measures accordingly.

User-Centric Design: Future directions in these security solutions will focus on user-centric design, emphasizing the need for solutions that are intuitive, accessible, and aligned with users' needs. Collaboration between security professionals, designers, and users will be essential in creating solutions that address both security requirements and customer experience.

Designing user-friendly security solutions requires a delicate balance between usability and protection. By adhering to principles of simplicity, clarity, and user-centric design, and by employing strategies such as risk-based and adaptive security measures, institutions can create solutions that are both effective and accessible. Real-world examples, such as password managers, MFA, and SSO, demonstrate successful implementations of this balance. As technology and user needs evolve, ongoing innovation and a focus on user experience will be crucial in developing security solutions that provide holistic protection while remaining user-friendly. Through thoughtful design and continuous improvement, organizations can ensure that security measures are both effective and seamlessly integrated into users' daily lives.

CHAPTER TEN:
PSYCHOLOGICAL RESILIENCE: BUILDING A STRONGER HUMAN FACTOR IN CYBER DEFENSE

Psychological resilience refers to an individual's ability to adapt to and recover from stress, adversity, or challenges. In the context of cybersecurity, it encompasses how well individuals and teams can handle the pressures associated with cyber threats, such as high-stress incidents, persistent attacks, and the mental toll of managing security risks. This chapter delves into the concept of psychological resilience, its importance in security, and practical strategies for building and maintaining it to enhance overall cyber defense.

Psychological Resilience: An Overview

Psychological resilience is the capacity to withstand and rebound from stressors or adversities. It involves several key traits, including emotional regulation, cognitive flexibility, and social support. Individuals who exhibit high levels of resilience are better equipped to manage stress, recover from setbacks, and maintain a positive outlook despite challenges. In the security sector, resilience is crucial because it helps personnel remain effective under pressure, adapt to evolving threats, and recover swiftly from security incidents.

Understanding the components of psychological resilience is essential for developing strategies to enhance it. The primary components include:

Emotional Regulation: The ability to manage and respond to emotions effectively. This includes maintaining composure during high-pressure situations, such as during a cyber-attack, and preventing emotional responses from impairing decision-making.

Cognitive Flexibility: The capacity to adapt thinking and problem-solving approaches in response to new information or changing circumstances. In cybersecurity, this means being able to shift strategies and approaches when faced with unexpected threats or evolving attack vectors.

Social Support: The presence of a supportive network that provides encouragement, advice, and assistance. For security professionals, this support can come from colleagues, mentors, or support groups within the organization.

Problem-Solving Skills: These are critical for resilience as they enable individuals to effectively address and overcome challenges. This component involves the ability to identify problems, develop and implement solutions, and evaluate the effectiveness of those solutions. In this setting, strong problem-solving skills help professionals tackle complex issues, such as security breaches or system failures, by systematically analyzing the situation, exploring possible solutions, and taking decisive actions. Effective problem-solving not only aids in managing current issues but also prepares individuals to handle future challenges more effectively.

Optimism: It plays a vital role in psychological resilience by influencing how individuals perceive and respond to adversity. Optimistic individuals tend to maintain a positive outlook, even in the face of difficulties, and believe that they can influence outcomes through their efforts.

Here, optimism can enhance resilience by encouraging a proactive approach to challenges and fostering persistence in the face of setbacks. Optimistic individuals are more likely to view problems as temporary and solvable, which can help them remain motivated and focused on finding solutions.

Self-Efficacy: Self-efficacy refers to an individual's belief in their ability to successfully execute the tasks required to achieve specific goals. This component of resilience is essential for maintaining confidence and motivation, particularly during stressful or challenging situations. In cybersecurity, self-efficacy contributes to resilience by empowering professionals to tackle complex tasks and respond effectively to threats. Individuals with high self-efficacy are more likely to take initiative, persevere through difficulties, and adapt to changing circumstances, all of which are crucial for maintaining effective cyber defense.

Psychological resilience plays a pivotal role in ensuring security by impacting various dimensions of performance and effectiveness. Resilient individuals and teams are better equipped to manage the intense stress associated with cyber threats, adapt to evolving challenges, and recover from setbacks. One of the fundamental ways resilience strengthens this concept is through stress management. Handling high-pressure situations, such as responding to a cyberattack, requires a calm and collected approach. Resilient professionals can maintain their composure under stress, which is crucial for making sound decisions and executing effective responses during incidents.

Another significant aspect is adaptability. The cyber landscape is continually evolving, with new threats and vulnerabilities emerging regularly. Resilient individuals and teams are able to adjust their strategies and tactics in response to these changes, ensuring that defenses remain robust and effective. This cognitive flexibility allows for a proactive rather than reactive approach to security, enabling teams to stay ahead of potential threats and swiftly implement new measures as needed. Recovery from setbacks is another critical role of resilience. Security breaches or failures can be demoralizing, but resilient professionals are able to bounce back from these setbacks. They use these experiences as learning opportunities to improve their processes and responses. This recovery aspect not only helps in restoring normal operations but also in refining strategies and strengthening defenses to prevent future incidents.

Enhanced Problem-Solving is an additional benefit of psychological resilience. Individuals who are resilient approach problems with a constructive mindset, which is essential in cybersecurity where complex issues frequently arise. Their ability to systematically analyze problems, develop effective solutions, and execute these solutions effectively contributes to better incident handling and more robust defenses. Optimistic professionals view challenges and threats as opportunities for growth rather than insurmountable obstacles. This positive outlook fosters a proactive approach to addressing issues, encouraging continuous improvement and innovation. By maintaining a hopeful perspective, individuals are more likely to persevere through difficult situations and remain committed to enhancing security measures. Resilient individuals with strong self-efficacy are more likely to tackle complex problems with assurance, take initiative in high-pressure situations, and adapt to new challenges. This self-belief enhances their overall effectiveness and contributes to a more secure and resilient organizational posture.

Developing psychological resilience involves cultivating specific skills and practices that enhance an individual's ability to cope with and recover from stress. Here are several strategies for building resilience in cybersecurity professionals:

Stress Management Techniques: Effective stress management is fundamental to resilience. Techniques such as mindfulness, meditation, and deep-breathing exercises can help individuals manage acute stress and maintain mental clarity. For example, regular mindfulness practice can improve focus and reduce anxiety, which is particularly beneficial during high-stress situations like a cyberattack.

Cognitive Behavioral Strategies: Cognitive Behavioral Therapy (CBT) techniques can help individuals reframe negative thoughts and develop more adaptive thinking patterns. In this setting, CBT can assist professionals in managing the cognitive distortions that might arise during stressful incidents, such as catastrophizing or overgeneralizing. By challenging these negative thought patterns, individuals can maintain a more balanced perspective and approach problems more effectively.

Building a Supportive Network: Establishing a strong support network within the organization can significantly enhance resilience. This network should include mentors, peers, and supervisors who can provide guidance, encouragement, and practical support. Regular team meetings and debriefings also foster a sense of community and shared purpose, helping individuals feel less isolated during challenging times.

Training and Skill Development: Continuous training and skill development are crucial for building resilience. By staying current with the latest security practices and technologies, professionals can feel more confident and prepared to handle emerging threats. Regular drills and simulations can also help individuals and teams practice their response to cyber incidents, enhancing their ability to manage stress and adapt to high-pressure situations.

Cultivating a Resilient Cybersecurity Culture

Fostering a resilient culture within an organization involves more than just individual strategies; it requires creating an environment that supports and encourages resilience across the board.

Leadership support is foundational to this effort. Leaders set the tone for the organizational culture and play a crucial role in modeling resilient behaviors. By demonstrating resilience through their actions, providing resources, and offering consistent support, leaders can inspire and motivate their teams. Effective leadership also involves creating a transparent environment where challenges can be openly discussed, and where employees feel encouraged to seek help and share their experiences. Clear communication is another critical element in building a resilient cybersecurity culture. Open and transparent communication ensures that all team members are informed and aligned, reducing uncertainty and confusion during high-pressure situations. Effective communication involves not only regular updates and information sharing but also actively listening to feedback from employees. This practice helps to build trust and ensures that everyone is on the same page, which is essential for coordinating responses to security incidents and fostering a cohesive team environment.

Promoting a growth mindset is integral to cultivating resilience. A growth mindset encourages individuals to view challenges and setbacks as opportunities for learning and development rather than as insurmountable problems. This perspective fosters a proactive approach to overcoming obstacles and drives continuous improvement. In a resilient security culture, employees are encouraged to embrace learning opportunities, seek out new skills, and view failures as a chance to refine their strategies and enhance their capabilities. Lastly, recognition and reward play a significant role in reinforcing resilience. Acknowledging and celebrating resilience and effective performance not only motivates individuals but also highlights its value within the organization. Recognitions can take many forms, from formal awards and public acknowledgments to informal praise and constructive feedback. By recognizing and rewarding resilient behaviors, organizations reinforce the importance of these traits and encourage others to adopt similar approaches.

Together, leadership support, clear communication, a growth mindset, and recognition and reward contribute to a culture where resilience is valued and promoted. Such an environment not only enhances individual and team performance but also strengthens the organization's overall ability to handle and recover from cybersecurity challenges.

Practical Applications and Case Studies

Understanding the practical application of resilience-building strategies and examining relatable case studies can provide valuable insights into their effectiveness.

Case Study 1: The Impact of Stress Management Training

A financial services firm implemented a comprehensive stress management training program for its cybersecurity team. The program included mindfulness workshops, stress management seminars, and individual coaching sessions. Post-training evaluations revealed significant improvements in stress levels, job satisfaction, and overall performance. The team reported enhanced focus, reduced burnout, and a more positive outlook, demonstrating the effectiveness of stress management techniques in building resilience.

Case Study 2: Cognitive Behavioral Therapy in Cybersecurity

A tech company introduced CBT-based workshops for its security analysts to help them manage stress and improve their problem-solving skills. The workshops focused on identifying and challenging negative thought patterns and developing more adaptive coping strategies. Analysts who participated in the program reported improved confidence, better stress management, and more effective responses to security incidents. The program highlighted the benefits of cognitive behavioral strategies in enhancing resilience and performance.

Case Study 3: Building a Supportive Cybersecurity Culture

An international cybersecurity firm prioritized creating a supportive culture by implementing regular team debriefings, providing mentorship opportunities, and fostering open communication. The company also introduced resilience training and recognized employees who demonstrated exceptional resilience during high-pressure situations. The results included increased team cohesion, reduced turnover, and improved response times during cyber incidents. The case study underscores the importance of a supportive culture in fostering resilience and enhancing overall effectiveness.

While building psychological resilience is crucial, several challenges and limitations must be addressed. These include:

Overcoming Resistance to Resilience Training: Some individuals may resist resilience training or perceive it as an unnecessary burden. Addressing these concerns involves clearly communicating the benefits of resilience training and integrating it into professional development programs. Providing evidence of its positive impact and ensuring that training is practical and relevant can help overcome resistance.

Managing Resource Constraints: Organizations may face resource constraints when implementing resilience-building programs. Prioritizing key initiatives, leveraging existing resources, and seeking external support can help address these limitations. Additionally, integrating resilience practices into existing training and development programs can make the process more efficient and cost-effective.

Balancing Resilience and Workload: While building resilience is important, it is essential to balance it with manageable workloads. Overloading employees with excessive responsibilities can counteract the benefits of resilience training and lead to burnout. Ensuring a reasonable workload, providing adequate support, and promoting work-life balance are crucial for maintaining resilience and overall well-being.

Building psychological resilience is a critical component of enhancing the human factor in cyber defense. By understanding the components of resilience, implementing effective strategies, and fostering a supportive culture, organizations can improve their ability to handle stress, adapt to changing threats, and recover from setbacks. Practical case studies demonstrate the practical benefits of resilience-building initiatives, highlighting their impact on performance and well-being.

Addressing challenges and limitations ensures that resilience efforts are effective and sustainable. Ultimately, a resilient cybersecurity workforce is better equipped to navigate the complexities of the cyber niche, contributing to a stronger and more secure defense against evolving threats.

CHAPTER ELEVEN:
ETHICAL CONSIDERATIONS: PRIVACY, MANIPULATION AND SECURITY AWARENESS

Ethical considerations are critical in guiding how organizations and individuals approach privacy, manipulation, and security awareness. As technology advances and cyber threats become more sophisticated, the balance between effective security measures and ethical principles becomes increasingly complex. This chapter explores the ethical dimensions of cybersecurity, focusing on three main areas: privacy, manipulation, and security awareness. It delves into the challenges and considerations inherent in these areas, and offers insights into how ethical practices can be maintained while addressing the demands of modern security infrastructure.

Privacy: Balancing Security and Personal Rights

Privacy is a fundamental human right and a cornerstone of ethical security practices. However, the need to protect digital assets and data often puts privacy at risk, creating a delicate balance between security measures and individual rights. We will examine them under these sections namely privacy, manipulation and security awareness.

Privacy in Cybersecurity

Privacy is a core aspect of ethical cybersecurity practices, serving as a critical pillar in safeguarding individual rights and maintaining trust. As organizations increasingly collect, process, and store personal data, protecting this data while upholding privacy rights becomes essential. Ensuring privacy involves implementing robust data protection measures, such as encryption, access controls, and secure data handling practices. This commitment to privacy is not only a legal obligation but also a key factor in building and maintaining trust with customers and stakeholders.

One of the primary reasons for emphasizing privacy in this context is to comply with legal and regulatory requirements. Various regulations, such as the General

Data Protection Regulation (GDPR) in the European Union and the California Consumer Privacy Act (CCPA) in the United States, mandate strict guidelines for data protection and privacy. Non-compliance with these regulations can result in severe penalties, legal actions, and reputational damage. Adhering to these laws ensures that organizations are not only protecting personal data but also avoiding legal repercussions. Maintaining privacy is crucial for preserving the trust and reputation of an institution. When personal data is mishandled or exposed, it can lead to significant damage to an organization's reputation, eroding customer confidence and loyalty. By prioritizing privacy and demonstrating a commitment to safeguarding personal information, organizations can build stronger relationships with their customers and enhance their overall reputation. Trust is a valuable asset in the digital age, and protecting privacy plays a pivotal role in earning and retaining it.

Effective personal security practices contribute to better risk management by reducing the likelihood of data breaches and unauthorized access. Implementing strong privacy measures, such as data encryption and access controls, mitigates the risk of data exposure and protects against potential threats. By proactively managing these risks, organizations can prevent costly data breaches and ensure that personal information remains secure. This approach not only protects individuals' data but also reduces the financial and operational impact of potential security incidents. Beyond legal and business considerations, upholding privacy reflects a company's ethical responsibility. Respecting individuals' privacy rights is a fundamental ethical principle, and organizations have a duty to handle personal data with care and integrity. This ethical commitment involves being transparent about data practices, obtaining informed consent, and ensuring that data is used only for its intended purpose. Upholding privacy as an ethical standard demonstrates respect for individuals and reinforces the organization's commitment to ethical practices.

Protecting privacy can also enhance the overall user experience. When individuals know that their personal data is handled with care and respect, they are more likely to engage with digital platforms and services. Privacy-conscious practices, such as clear data policies and secure data handling, contribute to a positive user experience by fostering confidence and reducing concerns about data misuse. A strong focus on privacy can lead to greater user satisfaction and increased engagement with the organization's services. Strong confidentiality measures are critical in preventing identity theft, a serious consequence of data breaches. Personal information, when exposed, can be misused for fraudulent activities, leading to identity theft and financial loss for individuals. By implementing stringent privacy protections, institutions can help prevent such occurrences and safeguard individuals' personal identities. This preventative approach not only protects users but also reduces the potential for significant financial and legal repercussions for the organization.

These practices support the principle of data minimization, which involves collecting and retaining only the data that is necessary for specific purposes. Adopting data minimization practices reduces the amount of personal information at risk and limits exposure in the event of a data breach. By focusing on collecting only the essential data, organizations can better protect individual privacy and enhance overall data security. This approach aligns with best practices in data protection and reinforces a commitment to responsible data handling.

Privacy practices facilitate compliance with data subject rights, such as the right to access, correct, or delete personal data. Regulations like GDPR grant individuals these rights, and organizations must have processes in place to address requests related to their data. Ensuring that privacy practices support these rights allows organizations to respond effectively to data subject requests and maintain compliance with legal requirements. This not only demonstrates a commitment to privacy but also enhances the organization's ability to manage data subject interactions.

In summary, the importance of privacy in cybersecurity extends beyond mere compliance and encompasses a range of considerations, including legal obligations, trust and reputation, risk management, and ethical responsibility. By prioritizing privacy, organizations can enhance user experience, prevent identity theft, support data minimization, and facilitate compliance with data subject rights.

Manipulation: Ethical Boundaries in Security Practices

Manipulation in cybersecurity involves influencing individuals' behavior to improve security outcomes. While these methods can be effective in promoting better security practices, they raise significant ethical concerns about autonomy, deception, and transparency. Ensuring that such techniques are used responsibly and ethically is essential to maintaining trust and integrity in security practices. Some of the techniques include nudging and persuasion, evading deceptive practices, transparency and accountability amongst others.

Nudging and persuasion are commonly employed to encourage safer security behaviors without resorting to direct manipulation. Techniques such as designing user interfaces to promote strong password creation or sending timely reminders about security best practices can subtly guide individuals toward more secure behaviors. Ethical use of nudging involves ensuring that these methods are transparent and do not exploit individuals' vulnerabilities. It is important that individuals are aware of the intentions behind such techniques and that their autonomy is respected. Deceptive practices, such as phishing simulations or social engineering exercises, can be useful for training purposes but must be managed carefully to avoid crossing ethical boundaries. Deception can lead to stress, anxiety, and mistrust if not handled appropriately. To maintain ethical standards, these practices should be conducted with clear communication, consent, and a focus on educational outcomes rather than causing undue harm. Transparency about the purpose and methods of such exercises is crucial to ensure that individuals understand and benefit from the training.

Respecting individuals' autonomy is a fundamental ethical principle in cybersecurity. This involves ensuring that persons have the information and choices needed to make informed decisions about their security. Ethical practices require that individuals are aware of and understand the security measures being implemented, including any potential impacts on their privacy or autonomy. Obtaining informed consent means that individuals are fully aware of how their data will be used and have the option to accept or decline security measures. This approach supports transparency and respects personal decision-making.

Gamification, the use of game-like elements in non-game contexts, is increasingly used in security training to engage users and promote secure behaviors. While gamification can make learning more enjoyable and effective, it also raises ethical concerns. For example, if game elements are designed to manipulate user behavior in ways that are not fully transparent or that exploit psychological vulnerabilities, it can cross ethical boundaries. Ensuring that these strategies are implemented in a way that is honest, respectful, and aligned with ethical standards is essential for maintaining trust and effectiveness. Transparency and accountability are critical when implementing any form of manipulation or influence in security measures. Organizations should be clear about the goals, methods, and potential impacts of their security practices. This includes providing information about the rationale behind nudging techniques, training exercises, or other interventions. Accountability involves taking responsibility for the outcomes of these practices and being open to feedback from individuals affected by them. Establishing clear guidelines and oversight mechanisms helps ensure that manipulation techniques are used ethically and responsibly.

Striking the right balance between effectiveness and ethics is a central challenge in cybersecurity. While techniques such as nudging and gamification can improve security behaviors, it is essential to consider their ethical implications and ensure that they do not undermine individuals' rights or autonomy. Effective practices should be designed with ethical considerations in mind, aiming to enhance security without compromising integrity or trust. Regularly reviewing and evaluating these practices helps ensure that they remain aligned with both ethical standards and security goals.

Cultural sensitivity and respect for diverse perspectives are important considerations when implementing manipulation techniques in security mechanisms. Different cultures may have varying views on privacy, autonomy, and acceptable practices. Ethical security practices should account for these differences and avoid using techniques that may be perceived as intrusive or disrespectful in certain cultural contexts. Engaging with diverse groups and considering cultural factors in the design and implementation of security practices helps ensure that they are ethical and inclusive. Addressing ethical boundaries in employing manipulation involves careful consideration of nudging and persuasion techniques, avoiding deceptive practices, respecting autonomy and informed consent, and balancing effectiveness with ethics. Incorporating transparency, accountability, and cultural sensitivity into these practices ensures that they are implemented responsibly and ethically. By navigating these ethical considerations thoughtfully, organizations can enhance security while maintaining trust and respect for individuals.

Security Awareness: Educating Without Overstepping

Security awareness is a cornerstone of effective cybersecurity, aimed at equipping individuals with the knowledge and skills necessary to recognize and respond to cyber threats. Properly designed security awareness programs help mitigate risks by educating users about potential threats and best practices. However, creating such programs involves careful ethical considerations to ensure they are both effective and respectful of participants' privacy and autonomy.

An effective security awareness program should be engaging, relevant, and respectful of participants. Training should cover essential topics such as recognizing phishing attempts, using strong passwords, and understanding safe internet practices. However, it's crucial that this training is designed to be user-friendly and avoids overwhelming individuals with excessive information. Effective programs utilize interactive elements, real-world scenarios, and practical advice to keep participants engaged while ensuring that the information is accessible and applicable. The psychological impact of these awareness training is an important consideration. Training programs should aim to inform and empower without causing undue stress or fear. Overloading individuals with alarming statistics or fear-based tactics can lead to anxiety and resistance rather than constructive behavior change. Instead, programs should focus on building confidence and providing practical, actionable steps that persons can take to protect themselves. Balancing education with positive reinforcement helps maintain a supportive learning environment and encourages proactive behavior.

Regular evaluation and adjustment of security awareness programs are essential to their ongoing effectiveness and ethical alignment. Organizations should seek feedback from participants to understand what aspects of the training are working well and which areas may need improvement. This feedback loop allows for continuous refinement of the program to better meet the needs of users and address any concerns that arise. By staying responsive to participant feedback and evolving security threats, companies can ensure that their training remains relevant and effective.

These awareness programs should be designed with inclusivity and accessibility in mind. This means providing training materials and resources that are accessible to individuals with diverse needs and abilities. For example, offering materials in multiple languages, providing accommodations for individuals with disabilities, and ensuring that content is understandable for people with varying levels of technical expertise are all important considerations. An inclusive approach ensures that all employees can benefit from security training and helps to create a more equitable learning environment. Given the rapidly changing landscape of cybersecurity threats, it is crucial for security awareness programs to be regularly updated. New threats and vulnerabilities emerge frequently, and training content must reflect the latest information and best practices. Regular updates help keep participants informed about current risks and ensure that they are prepared to handle new types of cyber threats. An up-to-date program maintains relevance and effectiveness, ensuring that users are equipped with the latest knowledge to protect themselves and their organizations.

People have diverse learning styles, and effective security awareness training should accommodate these differences. Incorporating a variety of teaching methods, such as visual aids, interactive simulations, and hands-on exercises, can help engage participants with different preferences. By catering to different learning styles, organizations can enhance the effectiveness of their training and ensure that the information is absorbed and retained by a broader audience. This approach increases the likelihood that participants will apply the knowledge in practical situations. In summary, security awareness training plays a critical role in enhancing cybersecurity by educating individuals about potential threats and best practices. Designing effective and respectful programs, addressing psychological impact, evaluating and adjusting training approaches, ensuring inclusivity and accessibility, providing regular updates, and engaging different learning styles are all essential components of a successful security awareness strategy. By addressing these aspects thoughtfully, organizations can build a strong foundation for improved security practices and a more resilient defense against cyber threats.

Case Studies and Examples

Examining real-world examples can provide insight into the ethical challenges and solutions related to privacy, manipulation, and security awareness in cybersecurity.

Case Study 1: Privacy Concerns in Data Breaches

A notable case is the 2017 Equifax data breach, where sensitive personal information of over 147 million people was exposed. The breach highlighted the importance of privacy and data protection. Equifax faced criticism for its handling of the breach and its response to affected individuals. The case underscores the need for robust data protection measures and transparent communication with individuals about data breaches and their implications.

Case Study 2: Ethical Boundaries in Phishing Simulations

In a 2019 incident, a company's phishing simulation exercise led to significant distress among employees. The simulation was conducted without prior notice or clear communication, resulting in feelings of anxiety and mistrust. This case illustrates the importance of managing deceptive practices ethically, ensuring that simulations are conducted transparently, and focusing on educational outcomes rather than causing unnecessary harm.

Case Study 3: Successful Security Awareness Training

A leading tech firm implemented a comprehensive security awareness training program that included interactive modules, practical tips, and regular updates. The program was well-received by employees and resulted in improved security practices and reduced incidents of phishing attacks. This case highlights the benefits of designing respectful and engaging training programs that effectively educate individuals while respecting their privacy and autonomy.

Navigating the ethical challenges in this sector requires a thoughtful approach and a commitment to principles of fairness, transparency, and respect for individual rights.

These objectives can be achieved through some of these measures.

Developing Ethical Guidelines and Policies: Organizations should establish clear ethical guidelines and policies that address privacy, manipulation, and security awareness. These guidelines should outline acceptable practices, provide guidance on obtaining consent, and ensure transparency in data collection and use. Developing and enforcing ethical standards helps create a framework for decision-making and ensures that cybersecurity practices align with organizational values and legal requirements.

Promoting a Culture of Ethics and Accountability: Fostering a culture of ethics and accountability within the institution is crucial for addressing ethical challenges effectively. This involves encouraging open discussions about ethical concerns, providing training on ethical practices, and holding individuals accountable for their actions. By promoting ethical behavior and creating an environment where concerns can be raised and addressed, organizations can better navigate the complexities of security particularly in digital infrastructures.

Engaging with Stakeholders: Engaging with stakeholders, including employees, customers, and regulatory bodies, helps ensure that ethical considerations are incorporated into cybersecurity practices. Regular consultations and feedback mechanisms allow organizations to understand and address the concerns of various stakeholders. This engagement contributes to more ethical decision-making and helps build trust with those affected by security measures.

Ethical considerations in cybersecurity are essential for ensuring that privacy, manipulation, and security awareness are handled in a manner that respects individual rights and fosters trust. Balancing the need for effective security measures with ethical principles requires careful thought and adherence to best practices. By addressing privacy concerns, avoiding manipulative practices, and designing respectful security awareness programs, organizations can navigate the complexities of security in a digital environment while upholding ethical standards. Relatable case studies provide valuable insights into the challenges and solutions associated with these ethical considerations, underscoring the importance of integrating ethical practices into security strategies. Ultimately, a commitment to ethical principles enhances not only the effectiveness of security efforts but also the overall integrity and trustworthiness of the organization.

CHAPTER TWELVE:
FUTURE DIRECTIONS

As the digital sphere continues to evolve, the role of human factors in cybersecurity becomes increasingly pivotal. Understanding how behavior, cognitive biases, risk perception, and other psychological elements influence security practices is essential for developing effective strategies and solutions. The future of cybersecurity will be deeply intertwined with the ways in which human behavior and technological advancements interact, requiring a nuanced approach to managing and mitigating risks.

Human behavior is not static; it evolves with changes in technology, societal norms, and individual experiences. As digital tools and platforms advance, so too must our understanding of how these changes impact behavior and security practices. This dynamic nature of human behavior means that future research and strategies must continuously adapt to new technological innovations and social trends. For example, advancements in artificial intelligence, machine learning, and the Internet of Things (IoT) introduce new complexities and opportunities in this niche. These technologies not only enhance security but also create new vulnerabilities. Therefore, understanding how these advancements influence user behavior and security practices is crucial. As AI-driven security solutions become more prevalent, they will alter user expectations and interactions with security measures, necessitating a reevaluation of how users perceive and engage with these technologies.

Social norms and expectations surrounding digital privacy and security are also continuously shifting. As societal attitudes evolve, so do the expectations for how personal data should be handled and protected. The future of this industry must address these changing norms by adapting security practices accordingly. Emerging concerns related to data privacy, consent, and transparency in an increasingly connected world will need to be addressed. Organizations will need to be proactive in aligning their practices with these evolving expectations to maintain trust and compliance.

To effectively navigate the intersection of human behavior and cybersecurity, a deeper understanding of cognitive and behavioral research is essential. Insights from psychology, behavioral economics, and neuroscience can inform the design of more effective security strategies and solutions that align with human cognitive processes and behavioral patterns. For instance, advancements in behavioral research offer valuable insights into how individuals make security-related decisions and respond to threats. Future research should focus on understanding cognitive biases and heuristics that influence security choices. Studying how individuals perceive risk in different contexts can help tailor security measures to better align with users' cognitive processes, ultimately improving the effectiveness of security interventions.

Integrating neuroscience with security tactics can also provide a deeper understanding of how the brain responds to security threats and stress. By exploring neurological factors that influence decision-making and risk perception, cybersecurity professionals can develop strategies that address underlying cognitive and emotional responses. This approach can lead to more targeted and effective security measures that resonate with users on a neurological level, enhancing overall security outcomes.

Innovations in user awareness and training will play a significant role in shaping the future of this sector. As threats become more sophisticated, training programs must evolve to address the unique needs of different user groups. Personalized and adaptive training programs that cater to individual learning styles and security behaviors are likely to become more prevalent. Leveraging data analytics and machine learning, organizations can create customized training experiences that address specific vulnerabilities and knowledge gaps. Adaptive training modules that respond to users' progress and performance can enhance engagement and effectiveness, making security training more relevant and impactful.

Gamification and interactive learning techniques are also expected to play a significant role in future security training programs. By incorporating game-like elements and simulations, organizations can make training more engaging and practical. Interactive scenarios that mimic real-world threats can help users practice and reinforce their security skills in a controlled environment. This approach not only improves retention but also increases the likelihood that users will apply their knowledge in practical situations.

As cyber threats become more sophisticated and persistent, psychological resilience will be crucial in maintaining a strong human factor in these strategies. Building resilience involves preparing individuals and organizations to handle stress, adapt to changes, and recover from security incidents. Future strategies should include resilience training programs focused on stress management, adaptability, and recovery. Providing support for individuals to develop these skills can enhance their ability to cope with security challenges and reduce the impact of stress on decision-making. Integrating resilience training into broader security awareness programs can create a more holistic approach to cybersecurity, supporting both immediate and long-term resilience.

Cultivating a resilient organizational culture is also essential. A culture that values security as a shared responsibility, supported by leadership and characterized by clear communication and a growth mindset, can foster resilience. Future efforts should focus on reinforcing these cultural elements to create an environment that supports and encourages proactive security behaviors. This approach will help organizations build a more resilient defense against evolving cyber threats. Balancing the need for security with respect for privacy and autonomy is a complex challenge that will require ongoing attention and innovation. Addressing the ethical implications of data collection and usage is critical. As organizations collect and analyze more data to enhance security, they must navigate the balance between leveraging this data for protection and respecting individuals' privacy rights. Developing ethical guidelines and practices for data collection, consent, and usage will be essential for maintaining trust and ensuring compliance with privacy regulations.

Manipulation techniques, such as nudging and gamification, can be effective in promoting secure behaviors but must be applied ethically. Ensuring transparency and respect for individuals' autonomy is crucial. Manipulation techniques should be used in a manner that is honest, respectful, and aligned with ethical principles to maintain trust and integrity. Additionally, emerging technologies such as artificial intelligence and biometrics present new privacy challenges. Evaluating their impact on privacy and implementing measures to protect personal information while leveraging innovation will be essential.

The future trends will be shaped by interdisciplinary collaboration and continued research. Bringing together experts from fields such as psychology, behavioral economics, neuroscience, and cybersecurity can lead to innovative solutions and comprehensive strategies. Supporting ongoing research initiatives that explore cognitive biases, risk perception, and behavioral influences can provide new insights and advancements. Public and private sector partnerships can enhance efforts to address current challenges by facilitating the sharing of knowledge, resources, and best practices. Such collaborations will help develop and implement effective strategies that address the evolving needs of the digital landscape.

The future directions of this concepts are deeply intertwined with the evolving digital world. Understanding the dynamic nature of behavior, advancing cognitive and behavioral research, innovating user awareness and training, and addressing ethical considerations will be crucial for developing effective security strategies. By fostering interdisciplinary collaboration, supporting ongoing research, and navigating the ethical challenges of emerging technologies, we can build a more resilient and secure digital future. The insights and approaches explored throughout this book provide a roadmap for addressing the complex human factors that will shape the future of cybersecurity, ensuring that we remain prepared for the challenges and opportunities that lie ahead.

ABOUT THE AUTHOR

Oluomachi Eunice Ejiofor is a distinguished cybersecurity specialist with extensive experience in safeguarding digital assets and enhancing organizational security. Eunice has dedicated her career to understanding the intricate interplay between human behavior and security practices. Her expertise spans a wide range of areas, including risk assessment, security awareness, and the psychological factors influencing cybersecurity.

She holds a deep commitment to advancing the field through innovative research and practical solutions. Her insights into behavioral factors and their impact on this niche have shaped effective strategies for protecting against emerging threats. As a thought leader, she has contributed to numerous discussions and publications, emphasizing the critical role of human factors in securing digital environments.

In addition to her professional achievements, she is known for her engaging approach to educating others about the field. Her work is characterized by a blend of technical knowledge and a profound understanding of the human elements that drive security practices. Through her writing and expertise, she continues to influence and inspire advancements, making her a leading voice in the field.

www.ingramcontent.com/pod-product-compliance
Lightning Source LLC
LaVergne TN
LVHW050841080526
838202LV00009B/307